PR
ISMA

"The name of the Albanian novelist Ismail Kadare regularly comes up at Nobel Prize time, and he is still a good bet to win it one of these days . . . he is seemingly incapable of writing a book that fails to be interesting."

CHARLES MCGRATH,
THE NEW YORK TIMES

"Kadare's novels are full of startlingly beautiful lines . . . bracingly original similes swarm with an apparent casualness . . . gloomy and death-obsessed, but also frequently hilarious."

CHRISTIAN LORENTZEN,
THE NEW YORK TIMES BOOK REVIEW

"Kadare's books reflect his country and are imbued with Albanian myths and metaphors . . . [giving] both the sense and essence of a totalitarian state in language that, while straightforward, is literary and often allegorical. . . . Kadare's body of translated work . . . demonstrates that he is deserving of wider acclaim and readership."

SEATTLE POST-INTELLIGENCER

"If only most thriller writers could write with Kadare's economy and pace . . . Kadare, magician that he is, offers just enough information for his readers to make myriad interpretations. He is the most beguiling and teasing of writers who understands that what may not be apparent now may well be in a distant future."

THE SUNDAY HERALD

"An author who richly deserves the Nobel Prize."

"Mr. Kadare, winner of the Man Booker International Prize . . . has more in common with the experimental-fiction writers Alain Robbe-Grillet and Jorge Luis Borges . . . we're gazing on a multilevel storytelling realm where, whether you are a student of Balkan history, a lover of Greek myth or a German taxi driver, the warning signs all say the same thing: 'Don't look back.'"

"Ismail Kadare has been writing fiction steeped in history from a front row seat in Albania for more than half a century."

"Kadare is inevitably likened to Orwell and Kundera, but he is a far deeper ironist than the first, and a better storyteller than the second. He is a compellingly ironic storyteller because he so brilliantly summons details that explode with symbolic reality."

"The intriguing Albanian master Ismail Kadare. . . . Kadare's authorial tone is invariably ironic and his fiction is playful, as if he has never lost sight of exactly how ridiculous humankind tends to be."

ESSAYS ON
WORLD
LITERATURE

Aeschylus • Dante • Shakespeare

ALSO BY ISMAIL KADARE

ISMAIL KADARE

ESSAYS ON
WORLD
LITERATURE

Aeschylus • *Dante* • *Shakespeare*

*Translated from the Albanian
by Ani Kokobobo*

RESTLESS BOOKS
BROOKLYN, NEW YORK

First Restless Books paperback edition February 2018.

Paperback ISBN: 9781632061744
Library of Congress Control Number: 2017944634

Text designed and set in Garibaldi by Tetragon, London
Cover design by Jonathan Yamakami
Cover image: "Prometheus Bound," by Peter Paul Rubens

Printed in Canada

1 3 5 7 9 10 8 6 4 2

Restless Books, Inc.
232 3rd Street, Suite A111
Brooklyn, NY 11215

www.restlessbooks.com
publisher@restlessbooks.com

CONTENTS

TRANSLATOR'S PREFACE

THERE WERE close to 750,000 bunkers in Enver Hoxha's communist Albania—enough to hold each of the nation's three million inhabitants. By the 1980s, these spaces had become dilapidated, garbage-ridden, and, in the case of my own neighborhood's shelter, a favored hiding spot during childhood games. Although no foreign attack ever prompted their use as places of refuge, the bunkers instead served the purpose of trapping the Albanian soul within the concrete and barbed wire of Enver Hoxha's regime for nearly fifty years. That any sort of art should flourish in so inhospitable an environment was unlikely. That this inferno of political repression and isolation could breed a literary genius of Ismail Kadare's caliber is nothing short of miraculous.

Winner of the inaugural Man Booker International Prize in 2005 and a perpetual contender for the Nobel, Kadare has written over twenty major novels. As its leading literary voice since the 1960s, Kadare is alone in the Albanian canon, with no forerunners and, so far, no successors. In his fiction and nonfiction alike, he brings an unprecedented level of sophistication to the Albanian language by elegantly joining together its two dialects, the northern Geg and southern Tosk, to achieve tremendous linguistic depth. After immigrating to Paris in 1991 and dividing his time between France and Albania, Kadare's literary creativity assumed a broader, European scope; these days, he is as much an Albanian as he is a European writer, fully integrated in the French literary scene. His current place in-between nations reflects the worldly scope that

Kadare was always able to achieve in his writing, despite leading a tightly confined existence during Hoxha's regime. Not only has he been both published and praised in forty-five major languages, but his work also encompasses a range of themes and styles with a dexterity that firmly places him among some of the twentieth century's greatest modernist writers: Vladimir Nabokov, James Joyce, and Milan Kundera.

The essays included in this collection are important documents of self-disclosure that guide us through Kadare's creative laboratory. The earliest essay, "Aeschylus, the Lost" dates to 1985, while Albania was still under communism, whereas "Dante, the Inevitable" and "Hamlet, the Difficult Prince" were written in 2005 and 2006 respectively—over a decade after the downfall of the communist regime. These essays treat world literature as a system of interconnected networks that extends beyond national boundaries. They also open up a window into Kadare's existential loneliness to show how the author, by connecting to the whole of world literature from a great distance, flourished in a climate as toxic to art as Hoxha's Albania. As Kadare reveals by connecting Albania and the Albanian culture to the tradition of world literature, no cultures or literatures are ever fully isolated. In the absence of immediate literary brethren, Kadare found inspiration and camaraderie by reading Shakespeare, Dante, and Aeschylus—writers distant in time and space—in Albanian translations, which he then cross-referenced with the original texts.

"Aeschylus, the Lost," "Dante, the Inevitable," and "Hamlet, the Difficult Prince" illustrate the hybridity underlying Kadare's creativity—how he traveled across the world through books and circled back to Albanian customs and culture. As a young boy, he tells us in "Hamlet, the Difficult Prince," Kadare copied Shakespeare's *Macbeth* by hand, making small changes here and there, and thus tingeing the foreign text with his own Albanian experience. The essays in this volume show Kadare forging similar ties across the world with other books he deeply admires.

The most obvious place where literary kinships are articulated is in "Dante, the Inevitable," which maps out the Italian author's ties to Albania. Ever ready to stray from realism, Kadare finds in Dante's *Inferno* a poetic creation that vividly captures the oppressiveness of Albania during communism and during the nineteenth-century Ottoman occupation. Kadare, who in novels like *The Palace of Dreams* and *Broken April* took it upon himself to recreate Albania's present and her history through allegorical devices similar to Dante's, made the Italian author his own, much as he had appropriated *Macbeth* as a child.

Kadare reveals that Dante is beloved among Albanians for somehow, from a bygone era, capturing the nuances of their plight. Aeschylus and the Shakespeare of *Hamlet* share a similar bond with the Balkan people. In "Aeschylus, the Lost," Kadare traces connections between the vengeance motif in Greek tragedy and the blood-vengeance customs still present in the Albanian mountains. Through such similarities, he advances a hypothesis that places the roots of tragedy in Balkan culture, particularly the deeply vivid funerary and marital rites of the region.

In the third and final essay in this collection, Kadare notes similarities between Shakespeare's Hamlet and the many young Albanian men and boys burdened by the need to avenge the blood of their loved ones. Kadare cites the Northern Albanian collection of laws, *The Code of Lekë Dukagjini*, to outline the rules to be obeyed in cases of blood vengeance. In a compelling modern-day narrative, Kadare recounts contemporary trials where blood vengeance has been invoked, Albanian men are charged with murder, and Hamlet's tragedy reverberates through the courthouses. The code of blood vengeance persists in the Albanian mountains, and its offspring of unwilling, Shakespearean executioners lives on to this day.

Kadare sees the reality of his world illuminated through the prism of literature. He has spoken at length on literature's unique landscapes and timelines, which often defy objective phenomena. These essays are literary journeys fundamental to Kadare's creativity. The reader willing to follow Kadare will be transported to Ancient Greece, Renaissance Italy, early modern England, and communist Albania. The lover of literature will readily discern how Kadare's understanding of these spaces is focused through the lens of his literary inspiration. These essays chart a map of world literature and its geniuses dating back to antiquity with such critical awareness, that we may soon see Kadare himself bookending this lineage of geniuses.

ESSAYS ON
WORLD LITERATURE

Aeschylus • Dante • Shakespeare

AESCHYLUS, THE LOST

WHEN YOU PULL OUT a volume by Aeschylus on an October day seemingly made for curling up and rereading something special, you know immediately if you have found the right day for this kind of undertaking. Aeschylus is one of those writers who does not suit just any day. He demands a certain frame of mind. You probably know of Aeschylus from your early youth; you might have studied him in school, or heard about him in cultural documentaries on television. In short, there is nothing novel about him, so reading, or, more precisely, rereading him, is the ultimate conscious choice.

In reality, the words "reading" or "rereading" seem imprecise in this case. Leafing through Aeschylus feels more like a creative meditation than a reading. In fact, it would be quite natural if during reading the book itself were to remain firmly shut most of the time.

Certainly, this sort of thing requires an unusual state of mind that cannot be mustered up at any time. And if instinct tells you that today is not the right day, it is better to return the book to the bookcase and bide your time until such a day comes along.

The pages that follow are notes about Aeschylus jotted down on different days. These thoughts will allow the reader to judge if they were written on the right kind of day.

It is natural to want to know how a writer works. What hours does he keep? Where does he write? In the case of ancient writers, whose entire lives have been enveloped in oblivion, this desire turns into an agonizing dream. Everything feels unreachable, nonexistent.

And yet, it was a human hand that wrote the eternal tragedy. Somewhere, a hand once held a writing instrument that stitched together tragedies—letter by letter and line by line. There must be a house on some corner where tragedy was first born.

What did Aeschylus's workroom look like? We do not know anything about it, except the most important piece of information: there were no books in it.

Aeschylus was the "father of tragedy," and one of the forefathers of world literature. Was his unique fate a great sadness or a blessing? It is impossible to know for certain. Much about Aeschylus is not known. We can only imagine that he must have had a workroom with something resembling a table, where he likely piled the black tiles on which he wrote with a sharp object. On another side of the room, he might have had other tiles, perhaps containing a monologue from a recently performed tragedy by Phrynichus, or a few translated verses from *The Epic of Gilgamesh*. Homer he must have known nearly by heart. This was all he had. The rest he had to create himself.

He had to have closed his windows during the cold season, when a murky light likely shined through his oiled window paper as if in a dream, simultaneously bringing him closer to and farther from the world.

Did that murky light color his tragedies? What would they look like if his windows had been covered by glass instead of oiled paper? Two thousand years later, the tragedies written from behind glass windows by the Englishman Shakespeare were no brighter. Quite the contrary, in fact. Was the dark north to blame for this, or was the darkness inside of Shakespeare?

Many questions and suppositions arise when leafing through Aeschylus. This is why reading him can feel richer when we close the book often.

Like every creator, Aeschylus probably liked to go outside at the end of his workday. Perhaps he went to the theater to discuss an upcoming drama or to resolve a complication regarding the latest performance. Or maybe he wandered around in the market.

The marketplace he encountered was large, with few people. The temples were scarce, too, and they were hard to tell apart from smaller, more mundane buildings lining the square. But from a landscape that appears empty to our eye, in his mind rose unprecedented tornadoes of thought and imagination.

In Aeschylus's time, photography was not available to freeze into memory the happenings of a month or a week prior, let alone more distant events. At the mercy of anyone's imagination and interpretation, events grew malleable to the point that they resembled the phantasmagorias conjured up in dreams.

The ordinary-looking Aeschylus, the one with a receding hairline whose likeness was captured in sculptures, conjured thoughts and creative deliriums large enough to circle the globe thousands of times. At the time, no matter how aware he might have been of his status, neither he nor anyone else could appreciate the full extent of his achievement.

Tragedy was in its infancy. It was still a workshop, and he was its architect, builder, and possible victim. What literary news could he share in the market or in the gathering place of theater actors? Maybe some part of Phrynichus's upcoming drama that, finally, the selection committee was allowing to be viewed? Or perhaps he gleaned news regarding his predecessor, Thespis (but the original conveyor of these reports was a questionable source: the itinerant merchant Y or perhaps the prostitute X, who claimed she was an old friend of the departed Thespis). Maybe he encountered a foreign traveler who accidentally heard thirty verses of an ancient Sumerian poem about a certain Gilgamesh—a poem about the horror of death. But the rest of the poem proved to be hard to find. Aside from Homer's poetry, this was the entirety of his literary tradition.

Aeschylus had to return to his workroom in the company of the ghosts he carried within. Tragedy was there, at his feet, with its foundations laid open, its blueprints not yet completed, with its railings and dust.

Was it happiness or sadness to father tragedy, a doomed creature that sallied forth into the world to live a thousand lifetimes?

Aeschylus begat tragedy in the broad sense in which we understand it today. Naturally, there were others before him, covered over with dust by time. There was the tradition of oral poetry among the Greeks and other peoples of the Balkans. Additionally, there were Dionysian parties and nuptial and funerary ceremonies, as well as dozens of other phenomena organic to human society that naturally produced drama. At the end of the day, as Czesław Miłosz says, "trees were writing their own *Divine Comedy* about the ascent from hell to the spheres of heaven long before Dante wrote his."

Undoubtedly, his contemporaries played an important part in his work. Their thirst for spectacle, their excitement, their applause, their silence, the large polemics on the eve of competitions, the fights before performances, the scandals—all these were present in his work. Over the years, due to the tiredness that comes with age, it got harder and harder to get the wheels spinning inside his brain. He needed motivation, and it would have been difficult to find a better source of encouragement than the distant racket of spectators that came from the theater. He was often annoyed by them, cursing them to himself, calling them brainless, thoughtless, and blaming himself for even engaging them at all, but in reality, he knew that he could not do without their noise. He could not function without their murmurs, fieriness, and sadness; in short, he could not do without the collectivity with which his powerful brain was constantly engaged in an exchange of ideas.

From behind his oiled window paper, passersby seemed like shadows. "These are the Greeks," he would say to himself from time to time, during those breaks when his tired mind sought inspiration. He plucked the Greeks from his immediate reality and turned them into characters for his tragedies. This transition from reality into fiction was no less burdensome than the imagined, literary transition from hell into the living world and vice versa. For this reason, the Greeks were unrecognizably disfigured in his dramas, and perhaps it was precisely in these moments of disfigurement that theater masks were first born.

But who were the Greeks? What was special about them?

No doubt many things about them were special. They had a beautiful country, with a pleasant climate, olives, sun, a marvelous language, and music. They were smart, ingenious, and adventurous. They had a sense of beauty, philosophy, a moral code, and a well-developed concept of democracy. They had a mythology, temples, and a belief in hell and fatality. Although at a first glance it might have appeared as if they did not need anything more, a day came when the Greeks were enriched by a new treasure.

Just as the man who after rain falls on him unexpectedly remembers the crimes of his youth, so the conscience of the Greeks was surprisingly awoken, and in its age of maturity the Greek nation remembered a crime it committed in its childhood. Eight hundred years ago, the Greeks had suffocated the Trojans in their sleep.

The Greeks' collective regret may seem affected, but the fact that this regret became the primary nourishment for ancient Greek literature is enough to render it believable. If you were to take out the rotting corpse of Troy from Greek literature, the canon would be diminished by at least half its worth.

Greek writers took it upon themselves to expunge this crime from the conscience of their nation. The crime was exposed from all angles by the Greeks themselves, without any pressure exerted by other nations. They revived the Troy they had once sworn to bury so deeply that no memory would be left of it; they exhumed it themselves, brushed off its dirt, and testified on its past as tenderly as if they were speaking about themselves.

It was an unprecedented exorcism, a shocking act, simultaneously liberating and emancipating. For the first time in the history of mankind, the conscience of a people was willfully undergoing such a disturbance. That this disturbance was sought-after signaled the nation's readiness to produce great literary works.

We cannot know what world literature would look like without Aeschylus. We only know that his absence would disrupt its balance greatly. What would Shakespeare's witches be like? What would the Englishman's *Hamlet* or *Macbeth* be like? Dramaturges would have had to devise other means for expressing the despair of human consciousness. They might certainly have found a compelling alternative, but their concoctions could never surpass what the great balding dramaturge discovered 2,500 years ago in his spare room without books.

A contemporary interpretation of Shakespeare might rewrite the apparition of King Hamlet not as that of a ghost, but as that of an intelligence agent from a neighboring country. The agent is masked as a ghost, sent to show the successor of the king that, according to the data at his state's disposal, the king did not die peacefully, but was murdered by his brother as a result of an oath. This hypothetical might contextualize *Hamlet* and satiate our curiosity. But very quickly we remember that it is inadequate, because the ghost is more substantial than a corporeal being. It is a more complete being because it embodies the whole process of doubt, the allegations of the prince concerning potential murders, the communal whispers that affect everyone, the premonitions, the fear, and the intoxicating influence of the neighboring country's counterintelligence.

If it is difficult to imagine world literature without Aeschylus, it is just as difficult, if not more so, to imagine world literature with the entirety of Aeschylus's work present. How high would the status of the dramaturge rise if we had more than eight percent of his work? It goes without saying that his status would rise proportionally with each new work.

The person who most suffered from the erasure of Aeschylus's work is Aeschylus himself. His loss was titanic, and because of it he is eternally two-dimensional—always both in light and in shadow. Aeschylus embodies the world vision of the Greeks: his life was inextricably embroiled in the darkness of hell. Since loss is such an integral part of him, no study of Aeschylus can ever be complete without accounting for this emptiness. It creeps in from all sides. There comes a time when night falls on any such study, and it is futile to try to uncover the way or ask for directions . . . No one will answer.

Aeschylus called his work and that of his contemporary writers fragments from the banquet of Homer. But in reality, Aeschylus, just like the other great tragic poets, sat at the table alongside Homer. It may indeed be the case that the entirety of ancient Greek literature fed off Homeric motifs, but we must not forget that the great Homer also sat at a table filled with delights from the past feast of Greek mythology: the collective work of people born in the dawn of world civilization. Drunken by light, these people created a series of creatures that were both terrestrial and celestial, dead and immortal, and awash in history, drama, and passion of the most complicated kind. This mythology filled the world with light, from Mount Olympus down to the depths of the sea, from the royal courtyards to the deep caves, and from the dark subterranean space all the way to the stars of the Milky Way.

Homer was the first to claim for himself part of the mythological banquet of endless epics, which once existed alongside one another and have gradually disappeared over time, leaving only a few scant titles such as *Nestoriada, Tebaida, Edipodia, Danaida*, and *Agamemnoida*. These poems spread across the Balkans as though they were a cosmic substance from which could be created miraculous systems and boundless universes.

For centuries, Dionysian parties have been considered a point of origin for tragedies, a thesis echoed with great authority by Nietzsche. This theory has been called into question lately, albeit somewhat tentatively. A cautious vein of thought finds fault with linking Dionysian parties to ancient tragedy when the two have so little in common. Even the use of masks, often cited as a significant connection between the Dionysian parties and ancient tragedy, might be a tenuous fastening point. Unlike the masks of the Dionysian parties, which always resembled animals, tragic masks were human.

The final problem with determining the genesis of tragedy has to do with the name itself: tragedy. In fact, the roots of the word, *tragos* (goat or buck) and *aide* (song), would have disappointed the great disciples of the tragic theater. Whether we like it or not, the goat somehow found itself in the midst of all this. A goat must have either been the prize won by dramaturges, or the animal sacrificed over the party. And yet, goats were mentioned in many of the surviving first-person testimonies from the period. Whether by chance or because the goat earned its place through spilled blood, the bovid found itself at the root of the most sublime artistic genre.

Those who call into the question the theory that tragedy came from Dionysian parties often go too far and end up denying tragedy an origin altogether. This is due to the mere absence of another explanation. The theory that ancient Greek tragedy is a social phenomenon with a specific chronological beginning does not exclude the possibility that tragedy might also be traced back to the distant root of all arts—the beginning without beginning.

It is tempting to declare the loud and wild Dionysian party the mother of tragedy, but these parties could just as easily have birthed musical comedy. Because they seemed a more tangible concept to academics, Dionysian parties unjustly supplanted two essential moments in human life: death and marriage.

Precisely these two rites, the funerary one and its helpmate, the marital one, are the true and unfairly denied parents of tragedy.

Friedrich Nietzsche came close to revising this backward thesis that puts the Dionysian parties at the origin of tragedy. Even though Nietzsche wrote that tragedy, like all art, was first born of pain, an emotion unsuited to the happy Dionysian festivities, the anticonformist Nietzsche did not catch this discrepancy. He also did not catch on when he revisited this assertion during his later years, when his brain was on the verge of madness and emitting its last few embers of genius.

More so than the study of ancient texts, witnessing Balkan funerary and marital rites would have given Nietzsche the needed epiphany about tragedy.

These two ceremonies, the funerary and the marital one, have been the core cultural institution of the Balkan people for millennia. Often called the mirror image of each other, the similarity between these ceremonies is no accident: it comes from the interconnection of life and death as unique phenomena that spill into each other. Marriage and death, likely the most traumatic and sacred moments in a community, also served as communal schools for aesthetic education. Happiness, regret, burdens, the kidnapping of brides, excitement, the revenge of the dead, and anger were all contained in a small surface, a stage almost. No other rituals have the same spiritual disturbance one encounters in a wedding or funeral.

In no other communal ceremony is a single character, the dead person, or two characters, the bride and groom, the center of attention. What did it matter that they were not speaking? They exuded a wide range of passions and thoughts. The participants of the ceremonies fully depended on them and imagined themselves in their stead—those who were married remembered their own happy or unhappy weddings, the unmarried ones thought about their own future weddings, while everyone else thought about how they would be grieved or avenged after their deaths. In short, the air seethed with drama.

This disorder, delirium, and self-identification must have been the first iteration of dramatic art. At times people needed to reexperience the delirium of standing alongside a wedding dress or a burial hole in the ground. Could this delirium be experienced without waiting for a future wedding or funeral?

Aristotle's famous "catharsis," that cleansing of the spectator that was carried out after every show through "fear and pity" (Aristotle's *Poetics*), happens only through prior preparation. Nowhere does fear and pity strike a person more powerfully than in a funeral rite. Eventually, season after season, the ancient people turned from funeral guests to spectators. They could go to the theater and experience the emotions otherwise only felt at life's extremes, when people confronted their fates. Much like a spectator who goes to the theater in order to imagine himself in the situations he sees on the stage, so others go to funerals to imagine their own deaths.

In no other part of the world are tragedy, marriage, and funeral rites as similar as they are in the Balkans. The similarity was particularly striking among the Greeks and Albanians. As Austrian scholar Maximilian Lambertz says, the Albanian wedding ritual is nothing more than a leftover from the old scenario of the kidnapping of the bride. The way the wedding guests are seated, the firing of rifles, the changing return path, and the various rules about tracking the wedding party's movements are all reminiscent of a kidnapping—except now it is all staged.

Even today similar customs remain, although now a car is often used as a means of transportation. No Albanian taxi driver is surprised when a bride's escorts ask that the route and final destination be changed, even though the proposed itinerary makes no sense.

Funerary rites resemble tragedies even more closely: from the way they were publicly announced, which in the absence of a postal service was done through yelling, to the self-inflicted scars on the mourners' faces, which resembled the masks of tragedy, and the professional women criers, who often read their lines like actresses.

Let us examine the funerary rites up close. They peak in intensity at the moment when the corpse is buried. The burial area is, without a doubt, nearly identical to the great tragic theater. It is an unusual space with its hole, or absence, in the middle. As the corpse is lowered into this absence, the boundaries between life and death are bridged. The main protagonist, the dead person, lives their last moments between two kingdoms. Despite their inanimateness, they are at the center of attention. Because they cannot speak, others, such as relatives and professional criers, have to speak on their behalf.

These criers were the first incarnation of the ancient choir.

According to August Wilhelm Schlegel, the ancient choir is the ideal spectator, a chosen elite that speaks on everyone's behalf.

Friedrich Schiller clarifies this further by adding that the choir is a type of living wall, which, while isolating tragedy, also protects her.

This is precisely the role of the criers. They are invited to witness death in order to articulate, in an ordered manner, the spontaneous and uncouth pain of those close to the deceased. Just as the ancient choir protected tragedy from the masses of spectators, so the criers protected the funerary rites from the family members and from blood vengeance seekers.

This sidestepping of the family's grief and its transformation into a public matter initiated the process via which mourning became a public institution.

The transformation of mourning could not have been an easy one. The burial ground must have witnessed many confrontations between mothers and sisters drunk from loss, and cold, professional criers.

Everything becomes clearer if we remember that in ancient Greek the word for "actor" is *hypokrites*, which really means liar, hypocrite—a fitting description for the professional criers who mourned death without having any blood ties?

To this day, in Albanian we use the expression "crying according to the laws." The word "law" in Albanian is the same as "to read," and when turned into a participle it can mean to sing a funerary song. "Crying according to the laws" means to cry as per a codified text.

Undoubtedly, the criers must have been condemned many times. Disgusted by their hypocrisy, relatives must have asked that the criers leave the grave site. The criers may have even considered abandoning their strange and sad performances, but the requests to display their odd mastery, and the offense that its false grief elicited, continued.

At that same scene, surrounding the burial hole, it became clear that the performance of grief was more interesting to an audience than unvarnished pain. One of the universal laws of art became manifest in these Balkan grave sites: by distancing itself from life and from personal passions, art renounces a shackled truth and takes on a heavier burden—that of creation. This distance makes for a fraught relationship between life and art. Homer famously verbalized this contentious relationship by saying that gods sent us misfortune in order to provide us with a subject matter for our songs. Schopenhauer similarly tiered art above life by declaring life an unworthy subject of art.

Rejecting the uncouth cry of a relative in favor of the cold, professional cry that has been filtered through technique or artifice was one of the foundations of art. Let us now imagine what would happen at the burial site of a man murdered over blood vengeance, a common enough scene in the Albanian mountains. According to the rules of the Code of Lekë Dukagjini, or the *Kanun*, the killer was obliged to participate in the burial of the victim by visiting the home of the deceased and sharing a meal with his family. To call this moment a dramatic one is, needless to say, insufficient. The drama connects everything together, as if these funerary rites were a theater of life.

The burial hole has haunted humanity throughout the course of history. That hole in the ground is where the value of the cold, artificial cry really came to light. The hypocrites wore masks that embodied estrangement. They paved the way for another kind of tragic mourning, in which they could imagine mourning someone else and even becoming someone else. Eventually, the criers got tired of the silence of the dead and began to dream boldly and sinfully of the dead speaking back. The return of the dead has undoubtedly been the greatest dream of the human species. Confronted with its impossibility, the great tragedians raised the dead from the grave and allowed them to testify on their demise.

This action had a dual scope. On the one hand, these things happened on the scene. But beyond the scene, funeral-goers become both mourners and spectators.

In his *Poetics*, Aristotle twice hints at the relationship between the theater and the funerary rite. In chapter four, he expresses the idea that "Objects which in themselves we view with pain, we delight to contemplate when reproduced with minute fidelity: such as the forms of the most ignoble animals and of dead bodies."

In other words, a theatrical performance could be seen as a continuation of the ritual, but this time the corpse, perhaps by now decomposed, is tolerable in our eyes because it is mirrored by an actor.

In chapter twelve, Aristotle speaks about the components of tragedy. Aside from the prologue, episode, exode, and the chorus, he mentions the commos. Chapter twelve of the *Poetics* ends with the phrase: "A commos is a joint lamentation between the chorus and one or more of the actors on the stage." The Albanian town of Gjirokastra still uses the term "cry with the world," meaning an intimate mourning in which non-relatives also participate. In his typically terse style, Aristotle does not provide further explanation. If he had added that the communal lament of the theater echoed the funerary ritual, he might have spared humanity the two-thousand-year-old torment that the murkiness of tragedy inspired.

Aristotle is notoriously terse at the end of chapter nine of *Poetics*, where he speaks of the statue of the athlete Mitys, which avenged itself by falling on the person who had killed the athlete. But the philosopher withholds any further commentary on the relationship between the theater and sculpture.

The statue, the mark, the tombstone, the corpse, and the actor are all as related to one another as they are connected to the theater.

The first statues must have caused a great disturbance by showing mankind a frozen, stony manifestation of itself. Ancient drama reverted this process by reanimating the frozen corpse on the stage. The unnatural movements under the heavy costumes, the white and chilling masks, the whispered voices—all of these made death seem more tangible.

Raising the first character from the dead could not have been easy. The ghost must have played an important intermediary step in all this. Older than any artistic creation, but no younger than most primitive objects, it was natural that the ghost would facilitate this artistic process.

For ancient Greeks, ghosts, nightly dreams, and prophecies constituted the liminality between people and divinity. As such, they played an important role in the transmission of omens from one world to another. In the tragic scene, where crimes were often covered up, the ghost served the role of the investigator, the witness, or the instigator of vengeance and remorse.

Jean-Pierre Vernant connects the origin of the ghost with the tombstone. The tombstone, long and raised, signals the resting place of he who has departed from the world. The tombstone was the dead's double, and shadow. Empty tombstones were even built in order to construct a tangible representation for those whose bodies were missing.

For the Balkan people, the tombstone, with its weight, silence, and coldness, was the silent placeholder for death. To this day, in Greece and Albania people swear "to this stone." To go back to Vernant, the expression "silent like a tombstone" retains its powerful meaning. The epithet "silent" contains an urging to speak that goes unheeded. "Silent" is a qualifier that can only be attached to an entity that *can* speak. The collective consciousness believed that tombstones were capable of speaking, just like a shadow or a ghost.

Under the moonlight the tombstones retained their silence, but eventually the great tragedians came along and forced their mouths open. They called the shadows to the stage so that spectators, with their hair raised in horror, could hear the dead testify.

Aeschylus not only borrowed from the Homeric and pre-Homeric table, he also added to the banquet the concept of justice, which was a key motif in the great tragedian's work. This preoccupation can be readily felt in *The Persians*, a play where it is clear that Aeschylus, who protected Greece as a soldier, is on the Greek side of justice. He universalizes the notion of justice. In his view, every human action calls the idea of justice into question. It is not easy to sort out what is fair and unfair, says his work. And, once you sort out which actions are fair and which aren't, it is nearly as difficult to align the audience's views with your own.

According to Aeschylus, what is just and what is right can contradict one another and thereby become indistinguishable. Tired, indifferent, and weak-spirited individuals may find opposing parties to both be right, but Aeschylus thinks "right" can only belong to one party.

The tragedian, however, does not consider justice static. For example, the excessive defense of your own justness can turn your motives unjust. The transferability of justice is evident in the Balkans, where, for thousands of years, people have killed each other in blood vengeance. The great tragedian, who not only knew but explored the issue of blood vengeance in *The Oresteia*, has given us the key to understanding Balkan blood vengeance. In the vicious cycle of Albanian killings, justice was perpetually transferred from one family to the next as they took and gave blood, all the while feeding death fresh corpses. The engorged passions of the Albanian mountains triggered a sequence of crimes that has spanned generations.

Among other things, Aeschylus's oeuvre warned people that transgressions against justice would not go unpunished, thus revealing the political element of his tragedies. Tragedy was populated by endless fights among people and lands, power struggles and bloody wars, the cries of winners and the cries of those who were defeated, ambition, vengeance, and the tragic positioning of the individual against his fate. In short, the tragic scene contained countless human passions and feelings that whirled around endlessly.

The ancient Greeks were well acquainted with the figure of the poet, the magician, the doctor, and the judge. It is irrelevant whether the judge was as prestigious as the doctor. The essence of his work was similarly bound up with hope and horror.

In various Albanian courts, where the question under discussion was blood vengeance and who owed whom blood, judges played a definitive, archetypal role. Their decisions, formulations, or compromises were transferred mouth to mouth like heroic deeds, connecting the judges, arbiters of the local code, with the tragedian. The judge was intimately tied to the doctor as well, since the doctor and the lawyer collaborated when determining the victim's cause of death in order to decide who was owed blood.

There is great discussion of the irregularities surrounding Agamemnon's death, particularly regarding the cape that immobilized the victim. An autopsy could have revealed a great many things at odds with the eyewitness testimonies.

A careful reading of *The Oresteia* reveals that Aeschylus was as much a poet as he was a judge. In order to account for justice so closely, he must have felt a profound sense of obligation toward it. The tragedian's active conscience gave his work its wide dimensions, tectonic power, darkness, and drama. Other writers, less burdened with such weighty consciences, find it more interesting to legitimize the transformation of a butterfly than to moralize about an empire.

An empire could house the fates of tens of millions of people, but some authors are willing to shut their eyes to this and insist on the drama of the butterfly.

Great writers respond to a different calling. Dante Alighieri could not have condemned part of humanity to the ninth circle of hell without sensing his own stature as a supreme judge.

There are many obstacles on our path to Aeschylus. Half a century after the tragedian's death, Aristophanes portrayed him as a passionate and proud figure. The inscription on his tombstone notes that he participated in battles against the Persians. This inscription, which oddly recalls the long hair of his antagonists, makes no mention of his work. Was this by accident, or was it proof of someone's secret desire that his work be lost?

What is known about his life is either meager or unimportant: he is blamed for exposing mysteries (the mysteries of theater, perhaps?) and he won two or three competitions (the last of which happened when he was sixty and *The Oresteia* came out). Shortly thereafter, he left Athens for Sicily, where he died when he was close to seventy. He reputedly died when an eagle, which mistook his bald head for a rock, dropped a turtle she had caught on it. Like many such stories about well-known people, this one may well be entirely meaningless.

As if the fog around him were not thick enough, a dark shadow covers Aeschylus and the majority of his tragedies. We come upon this darkness wherever we turn. It obscures all roads, reminding us that we know even less about Aeschylus than we do about Homer, for the latter at least managed to transmit to us his work in complete form.

The great absence of Aeschylus can neither be repaired nor filled in. But this erasure of his work is not the only thing keeping us from reaching the authentic Aeschylus. Even the little that has been preserved contains gaps and mistakes in transcription. This is perfectly normal given that these texts are the descendants of the copies of copies, written generation after generation by scribes from different periods. It is hard to imagine tracing these copies back to the original text, or even to the texts that were often distributed before the staged performances.

The ancient texts from which other ancient texts have been transcribed have their share of mistakes. The words are not separated from one another, punctuation is hardly there, and verses are filled out in prose. All of this makes the reconstruction of Aeschylus's texts extremely difficult. The rhythm of the verses and the grammar help somewhat in fixing the inadequacies, but not definitively so.

Lycurgus's decision to assemble a single text with the writings of the three great tragedians—Aeschylus, Sophocles, and Euripides—proves that official intervention was required to prevent the gradual deterioration of the text that could eventually cause catastrophic disfigurement.

The detrimental process of the copying and recopying the dramas of Aeschylus, as well as of his other great contemporaries, was not laid to rest with Lycurgus's resolution. This history is a long chronicle that dates back to the Roman and Byzantine publications—it is an eternal, frequently murky chronicle during which the slow erosion of the text continues at the hands of countless scribes, from century to century, until the unthinkable happens: the loss of most of Aeschylus's writings.

Scribes, the majority of whom were monks working in solitary conditions, would often change some words or verses from the works they transcribed in order to entertain themselves or to feel a sense of ownership over the text. Precisely when these scribes began to realize that they were not dealing with ordinary texts, but with the brilliant work of a genius writer, the tragedies started to disappear. This coincidence remains enigmatic.

We are, understandably, back to the loss.

How did it happen? No, it is not possible . . . These are the first instinctual responses to every loss, regardless of its nature.

How could ancient tragedies vanish?

When we lose a set of pearls in our house, we initially hope the loss is not permanent. Surely, the little box will be found somewhere within the four walls. We then turn the house upside down and search every corner.

The ancient tragedies were lost somewhere on planet Earth. The planet was quite small for such a monumental loss. Every corner could be searched, every archive, monastery, and library could be turned upside down. The tragedies, after all, had been lost here on Earth, and not amidst the stars.

This hope was pointless. They dug around for hundreds of years in every place the tragedies might have crawled into, but they could not be found. Even in its smallness, the planet was capable of huge losses.

The next question was: how did this happen?

As we mentioned earlier, the tombstone, which, according to Jean-Pierre Vernant, must have been the ghost of Aeschylus, had signaled the possibility that there would be loss. Did Aeschylus sense the black hole that would swallow his dramas? Surely, he must have. Every great creator senses when the work he creates is under the threat of extinction. The cliff was always two steps away, dark and foreboding by day and night.

The tragedies were written in several kinds of papyri. Except for those that would be given to actors, there were only a few existing copies of the original. If an enemy had decided to do so, he could have easily destroyed them all at a moment's notice.

But, because there would always be another copy in a safe place, this was not the main danger. There was a more serious threat: a drama by Phrynichus, *The Sack of Miletus*, was censored by the authorities because the show had bored the Athenians, reminding them of the horrors of the recently concluded Persian Wars. If we recall the angered Solon's dialogue with Thespis, it is clear that theater had its share of conflicts with censorship from the start.

The situation grew more complicated when official censorship was subjugated to the demands of spectators. The public engaged in its own crusade against tragedy, virtually ensuring that every great tragic trilogy would end with a fourth, satirical piece. This unnecessary addition, which foretold the later commercial obsession with happy endings, was a tax that the brilliant tragedians were forced to pay to contemporary taste.

Time birthed tragedy and therefore, naturally, loved it. But this love was not without its reservations, which were expressed in various ways. Opponents mandated the presence of comedy in every tragic creation. Plato's distaste toward the worshippers of theater reveals his reservation about the theatrical arts at large. It is not accidental that Plato valued poets about as highly as he did dream interpreters, or that he paired the art of tragedy to that of kitchen cosmetics. And if we turn to Socrates, we will detect a similar distaste.

Solon's angry departure from the theater cannot but recall another departure: that of Aeschylus from Athens. The departure of the latter evinces the coldness with which Aeschylus and his tragedy were treated. At a time when the number of tragedies could be counted on one hand, only a small step separated the repression of one tragedy from the obliteration of the entire genre.

The question of whether tragedy was necessary was raised many times by the ancient Greeks. It must have instilled in the minds of the tragedians fear similar to that felt by a twentieth-century Russian poet told that his songs merely disrupted the quiet slumber of his nation. The Greek tragedians had many reasons to believe that their works could disrupt the sleep of not only Greece, but of the entire planet. We now know that this was a necessary disruption.

Aeschylus's departure from Athens must have been the most pathetic moment of his life. In that moment, he must have shouldered the entirety of the great sadness future generations would experience over the loss of his work. He turned his back on Athens, the capital of the world, of light, and of theater. He left everything behind, including his plays. Bringing manuscripts with him was no easy task. Since they were written on plates or skin, the manuscripts of ninety dramas must have weighed at least several tons. Second, and most important, even if he could carry all this cargo, why would he do that? What good were they without the theater? He was losing them forever.

At a time when publication was not a possibility, dramatic works could not exist without the theater. The lifeblood of Aeschylus's dramas were wooden stages and the tragedian himself, for once he died his plays would no longer be performed. He whose titanic mind had imagined the downfall of gods, the clashes of laws, and the ephemerality of life must have known that his work, despite deserving to be immortalized, would eventually disappear. Greek democracy would not allow his books to be burnt, but time destroyed them as surely as any fire would have.

But how did this loss happen?

The question has been repeated throughout centuries, as questions without convincing answers tend to be reiterated.

More than one hundred years ago, a bright flame annihilated that which time would have taken centuries to destroy: part two of Gogol's *Dead Souls*.

The disappearance of Aeschylus's works has nothing in common with this violent destruction or with the slow oblivion of time that eventually envelops most human creations. Instead, there was only the accidental salvation of a small portion of tragedies. In short, it is not the loss but the salvaging that was accidental.

Loss is so closely bound to artistic creation, that the suicides of an endless succession of authors is often considered part of their artistic work, as though death were the final, ominous chapter of their literary trajectories. Loss is essential to Aeschylus's titanic work, and yet his loss was very particular. It was unlike the burning of Gogol's manuscript or the annihilation of Kafka's oeuvre.

Different scholars have tried to explain this strange phenomenon, but have been unable to do so convincingly. Some set the beginning of this chronicle of loss during the period of the Emperor Adrian, when certain works by the three tragedians were published. Aeschylus's *Prometheus Bound*, *The Persians*, *The Seven Against Thebes*, *The Oresteia* (*Agamemnon*, *The Libation Bearers*, *The Eumenides*), and *The Suppliants* were selected for this publication. These are the only tragedies that have remained.

Many consider it a miracle that seventeen of Euripides's tragedies were saved, when in the case of Aeschylus and Sophocles a mere seven of their tragedies survived. Was this truly a miracle, or was it something else?

It is likely that a sense of rivalry simmered between the three tragedians, and that the more serious and perhaps greatest writer among the them, Aeschylus, inspired the greatest animosity. We must remember here that even the scornful Socrates was willing to attend Euripides's plays. The verdict was gentler, then, on Euripides, who was willing to bring the theater closer to the people, and thus inadvertently brought about the end of tragedy.

Sophocles and Aeschylus led very different lives. Sophocles had a longer and easier life than Aeschylus. The latter, whose works and life were darker and more nebulous, was nearly entirely shrouded by time.

Let us return to the works, or rather to their loss. The long search for them uncovered two pieces, one from the satirical drama that ended *The Persians* and another from the *Hunters* by Sophocles.

What happened to the others?

According to some scholars, the publication of the selected dramas played a dual role. On the one hand, it saved the seven tragedies that we have today from extinction; but on the other, it helped accelerate the oblivion of the tragedian's other works. According to these scholars, by focusing on the seven dramas, history ignored core parts of Aeschylus's work (*The Seven Against Aeschylus* is how we might rephrase one of his titles).

In truth, it is hard to believe that reading *Prometheus Bound* in the Roman edition would spur the erasure of *Prometheus Unbound* and *Prometheus the Fire Bringer* rather than stimulating interest in these works. Likewise, *The Seven Against Thebes* could only have precipitated the revival of the Theban trilogy, of which only the one drama has survived.

It is clear that by saving some of Aeschylus's literary treasure, this publication could not have led to the loss of other parts. Between the fifth century BCE and the first century CE, time enveloped and erased countless works and authors. But while this erosion might affect more moderate works, time alone could not have destroyed true masterpieces.

Many scholars point an incriminating finger at monotheistic religions. After destroying the Greek gods, these religions wanted to subdue and efface all the literature where these gods appeared as characters. Nietzsche blames Christianity for this, but because of his personal animus toward Christianity he is unreliable in this attribution.

In truth, the light that came from ancient literature was in direct opposition with the dogmas of dominant religions. The deeper the darkness of the Middle Ages, the more threatening the light of the ancients became. It is no accident that ancient tragedy came to an end between the sixth and tenth centuries, during the early Middle Ages.

Dominion over the sky has been and will remain an ideological goal for many great religions. Monotheistic religions cannot conceive of sharing the site of human spirituality with another party. When the Greek gods were removed from the sky, earthly princes remained in the form of ancient writers and philosophers. But religion would not tolerate these Earth-bound sovereigns either.

To this day, the artistic merit of the Bible is compared with that of Homeric poems. These attempts tend to be ill-conceived, and the great Homer nearly always comes out victorious. Even Jesus Christ seems fragile and pedestrian when compared to the titanic Prometheus. Perhaps the most colossal elements of ancient Greek literature were erased by religion to avoid these sorts of doomed confrontations.

Instead of being subjected to witch hunts, dramas were slowly stifled and allowed to fade away. For centuries, monks and monasteries were the only shelter for thousands of manuscripts of worldly spiritual treasures. Eviction from these monasteries was a fatality. When one thousand ancient tragedies, the greatest treasure of humanity, found themselves banished, they were grievously, irreparably ruined. And what little the famous Alexandria library might have saved was burned by another faith, the Islamic one, this time in the name of its own Bible, the Qur'an.

And so began the long, monotonous history of handwritten copies, of mistakes, of forgetfulness, of rewording, and of textual alterations. After twenty-five hundred years of this majestically sad chronicle, all that remains of Aeschylus's universe are a mere seven dramas.

On an October afternoon, you fantasize about discovering even a small fragment of the lost ancient treasure. You think of how the event would be captured by TV cameras, and it suddenly seems like the kind of news that would not fit within today's forms of mass media communication. You realize that it is too late for such discoveries, and set out to think of something more acceptable. You give up on actually finding the fragment and think up another scenario: perhaps you uncover an old folder, a scandal from the past when it seemed that something had been found but it all turned out to be a disappointment. You imagine the conversation on the news, the TV anchors' guesses, the false manuscript—and then you remember that no such thing ever happened. No finding, no falsifying, nothing. You realize that this story has been spoken of for about fourteen hundred years—you sense the excitement that has driven a lineage of people to think like you and suffer over this issue.

You suddenly get irritable. You wonder why falsifiers never attempted to replicate Aeschylus's work. It would have been a normal, logical, and moral falsehood. An investigation of this non-crime is in order.

This non-crime is a further loss—a kind of hopelessness surrounding a greater hopelessness, a darkness that threatens us all.

There has never been a scarcity of falsifiers in the world. True falsification masters have good taste and know where to invest their time. They have always been a good measure of what was or wasn't valued by any given historical period.

Undoubtedly born shortly after the invention of writing and painting—the first written page must have given birth to the first falsification—falsification became a way of documenting history.

Falsifiers' scope was broad: it extended to wills, archives, love letters, receipts, prisoner testimonies, novels, tombstone inscriptions, telegrams, paintings, poems, and treasure maps. In fact, the recent 'discovery' of Hitler's diary shows that falsification is not merely a thing of the past.

The lost tragedies, though, were never falsified. It was already too late for this in the twentieth century, but the time was ripe for falsification in the tenth century, when the interest in ancient tragedy revived and European universities were starting to open up, their departments and brilliant minds looking to permeate the darkness of the past.

While the falsifiers were perhaps kept from approaching Pope Urban II in 1095 because he was busy battling Pope Clement III, there was nothing to prevent them from approaching Pierre Abelard from the episcopal school of Paris in 1140. And even if Abelard was too preoccupied with the love entanglements that precipitated his castration, falsifiers might have still turned to Cambridge University, which, although newer, was stealing many students from Oxford. Or they could have knocked on the university doors in Italy, where there was talk that Petrarch had found a Homeric manuscript that he could not read. If they did not take the Italian scholars too seriously, they could have migrated to Vienna in 1365, or to Cologne in 1388. They could even have traveled as far as cold Sweden in order to sit in front of Jakob Ulvsson, who had helped fund the University of Uppsala in 1477.

Yet they did not approach any of these centers of knowledge. In the fifteenth century, ancient Greek was undergoing the revival, but the falsifiers still did not move. In 1600 there was still time for this, but even a century later, on the eve of European neoclassicism and at a time when the Scottish James Macpherson published the *Songs of Ossian*, they did not appear. Not even when they had evidence that this particular deception had turned out quite well did the falsifiers near the ancient Greek tragedies.

Every circumstance seemed to be bent in their favor. To claim that they had found fragmented scenes would have been believable, and temporal distance would have justified any potential gaps in their narratives. The leather manuscripts gave a wide range of choices to the falsifiers. Their falsification could be mapped out along one thousand years. Beyond this, if they struggled with falsifying the original, they could have falsified it in Latin or even in Arabic and blamed any fissures on an extended chronology of anonymous scribes.

The falsifiers must have thought about this issue in depth, weighed the risks and the benefits, and eventually decided that falsifying Greek tragedies was not worth the trouble.

They simply preferred to go back to inventing erotic correspondences between nuns, posthumous academic works, and scandalous memoirs of a lord or a prostitute. Falsifying a boring academic or Margot the prostitute paid well, but nobody was willing to pay for Aeschylus.

This all goes to show just how little effort went into finding the lost dramas. We have nothing left but to be grateful that seven of Aeschylus's works were saved. In fact, we should marvel at the fact that any tragedies survived at all, just like people marvel at those who miraculously escaped a massacre.

It often happens that that pain of loss is focused on famous names. In the case of Greek tragedy, it belongs at the top. In Aristotle's *Poetics*, Aeschylus, Sophocles, and Euripides are mentioned alongside dozens of others without any overt classification, even though the implication that there *were* others is clear.

The Poetics can be read in a variety of manners. One way of doing so is to consider the text a post-catastrophic wasteland of ruins, leftover stones, columns, and soot from hearths that have been unlit for years. As though they had been washed away by a dark waterfall, some names appear in *The Poetics* only once and then disappear forever. Sometimes, an author's name appears without mention of their work; at others, a work emerges without an author; and at times there is even a faint whiff of a drama devoid of a title or an author. This is, in short, a communal grave with no end and no beginning.

The explanatory notes that come with Aristotle's *The Poetics* provide little solace. We learn that a certain Theodotus wrote fifty dramas, none of which have been preserved. Another meteor of a writer, Astydamas, presides over an even deeper grave, in which 240 tragedies lie interred. Just as devastating are Aristotle's references to remarks he made in his own books—books that no longer exist.

There are no words for the endless, communal grave of Greek tragedy. This wasteland leaves us no remains from which to reconstruct vanished dramas. Did they come into the world before their time? Or perhaps their messages were delayed somehow?

Just like our bodies and our language, our minds are bound to the Earth. Our thinking, although it may appear unencumbered to us, is not much freer than a prisoner's taking his daily walk in the prison courtyard. Human logic is as limiting as a stone cell. In the end, it is possible that our inept questions do not merit a deep answer.

It is unclear what principle motivated the person who, by putting together the collection of tragedies, saved the existing dramas. The collection begins with *Prometheus Bound*, which may have been considered an easy introduction to the world of Aeschylus. But following the complicated *The Persians*, *The Seven Against Thebes*, and *The Oresteia* with a simple drama like *The Suppliants* calls into the question the above explanation. It is more likely that whoever assembled the collection picked *Prometheus* because it seemed to exemplify Aeschylus's artistic concerns. If this was the reason, it also explains why the entire Promethean trilogy could not be included. But we will return to this later.

Over the course of the years, Aeschylus's work grew increasingly more complex and found new dramatic creations and modes of expression. From the seven dramas, *The Suppliants* has the simplest construction, which makes scholars mistakenly take it to be an older work. But despite its simple construction, *The Suppliants* posed questions that the human race had wrestled with across millennia. The unwillingness of the fifty daughters of Danaus to marry their close cousins is evidence of the centuries-old reaction against endogamy, and is also importantly related to humanity's renunciation of polygamy.

The Balkan legend of the brother returning from the dead to bring his sister back home echoes this universal anxiety. "Vidh systur thinni gaztu slikan mög" ("with thy sister didst thou breed such a son"), laments one of the characters of the ancient Norwegian *Edda*.

The fight between mother and son with which the Balkan ballad begins is one of the most beautiful moments in world oral literature. The brother's excitement at the prospect of marrying his sister and satiating his transgressive desire, the mother's ensuing regret, her curse, and the dead brother's rising from the grave to condemn what has happened—all reveal the dramatic journeys that humanity undertook to establish what seems unmovable in our day: the prohibition of incest. This ballad of the Balkan people, an echo of the moment in which the Balkans distanced themselves from endogamy, is much more disturbing than Aeschylus's *The Suppliants*.

The ballad proves that these peninsular people maintained their talent for phenomenal artistic creation even in later periods. Yet, because the Balkan people did not have writers, these creations were never cultivated into literature. The Greek people also lacked writers, and, after knowing the bright light of ancient art, were plunged into darkness alongside the Balkan people.

This darkness was the result of an unexpected turn in the wheel of history, which stole from the Balkan people their freedom and their art.

The Earth has known enslavement of all kinds, but it is hard to envision an enslavement as oppressive as that experienced by the Balkan people. It was a sojourn into inferno, a darkness that went on for hundreds of years within which whole generations were born and died blind. As if to counterbalance things, the ancient light of bygone years was covered by total darkness. The Balkan people underwent a desperate psychic disturbance. People who had once understood the world as layered into life, death, and ascension were now deprived of everything high and spiritual. It was as if they had lost the sky.

A shadow hovered over the Greek and Balkan civilizations for quite some time. It had already attacked the peninsula twice before: once in the form of the long-haired Persians and two thousand years later in the form of the Ottomans. The Balkans were like a household that did not yet understand loss. They had experienced small robberies and misfortunes, but they had not known grief. Aeschylus may have been one of the first to sense the real sorrow that lay ahead for the Balkans.

"But this is only a game, archon."

"A game, but very soon we will see what influence it will have on the citizens."

According to Plutarch, Solon, angered by a drama that recreated events from the past, exchanged these words with Thespius.

Years later, *The Sack of Miletus*, a drama that depicted the recent Persian occupation of a Greek city, awakened a similar response. Both the performance and its prohibition are described as follows by Herodotus: "When Phrynichus composed and produced a play called *The Fall of Miletus*, the audience burst into tears and fined him a thousand drachmas for reminding them of a disaster that was so close to them; future productions of the play were also banned."

We have, then, a drama with a historical subject and a drama with a contemporary subject that both awakened the anger of the state. Inevitably, the following question arises: what did the Greek state prefer, ancient and historico-mythical subjects or more contemporary subjects?

It seems that for a long time Greek officials were divided on this subject. In the name of the state and never in the name of art, the scales of victory were moved at times in one direction and at other times in another. After every scandal, the opposing side would get its vengeance until, finally, those who found the historical subjects a lesser evil triumphed.

The use of the term "evil" might be odd considering we are speaking of theater, something the ancient world considered sublime. But we shouldn't forget that we are speaking about the state's assessment of drama. In fact, we are discussing the state's divided pro-tragedy lobby, which despite its internal contradictions, advocated in favor of tragedy and battled and opposed those who sought tragedy's demise.

The dangerous nature of drama never eluded the Greek state. In fact, the greater the ceremonies and the more brilliant the dramas playing out on the stage, the more vigilant the government became. Its eye did not forget that evil could lie behind the surprisingly beautiful verses, the actors' stately voices, and the majestic outfits and masks. The state, realizing it could not fully efface drama and its potential to incite revolt, chose what it felt to be the least threatening for drama.

Mythical themes, the state decided, were less threatening than more contemporary ones, and thus the majority of the tragedies produced at the time related this celestial subject matter. *The Persians* is a remarkable exception. And even though we do not know with absolute certainty how many other contemporary tragedies were written, we can easily surmise that they could be counted on one hand.

Reading *The Persians*, one can easily detect Aeschylus's effort to make the drama acceptable to the selection committee. Even though it dealt with contemporary happenings, the drama had mythical dimensions. The space in which the action took place, the Persian imperial capital, seems otherworldly. Similarly, the characters and their shadows are almost supernatural. One cannot sense Greece at all in the drama, even though at the time the Greek nation was on the brink of catastrophe and more caught up than ever in the passions, heroism, omens, anxiety, and fatalism that so drew Aeschylus as a creator. But the tragedian was obliged to abandon the eventful terrain he occupied in order to grant the tragedy a mythical dimension. From this distance, the passionate events, full of noise and blood, could be judged in a deaf objective manner, as though by a shadow.

"What could go wrong with a drama like this?"

"What could go wrong? Didn't we have enough problems with Phrynichus's drama? Is this not the same subject matter?"

"This one seems different . . . and we should judge them separately from one another. Greece needs this drama."

"I'm sorry to remind you, but there are plenty of others who are thinking about Greece."

These words were not really spoken, but perhaps the cold-eyed Aeschylus was nonetheless cognizant of similar murmurs, and the censorious mark they bore.

The proud tragedian might have been offended (was not such an offense what made him abandon Athens years later?). He could have said, to hell with all of you and your theater, it is my own fault for putting up with you. And he could have slammed the door and left.

But he didn't. And it was not a thirst for fame, fear, or some lost honorarium that held him back. It was something else—perhaps it was precisely the sovereign mentality we considered earlier.

Like every great writer, Aeschylus was conscious that in comparison to the state officials that regulated his work, he himself was vastly superior, and not only in the sphere of art, but in terms of morality, too. As such, he stood higher than any official, and the fate of Greece weighed on his shoulders more heavily than it did on the entire mechanism of the state.

So he swallowed the offense, edited out the more incendiary parts, and brought his play in front of the public for the sake of Greece, the Balkan peninsula, and the whole world. *The Persians* was the most patriotic of Aeschylus's works, a kind of memorial to the war of the Greek people against the invading Persians. At the same time, it was a collective world monument to the wars of many people against empires, like small Greece confronting the massive Persians.

As it often happens with ancient authors, assigning justice within the play is an act that assumes national and international dimensions.

Aeschylus's tragedy underscores how Greece was being attacked by a tyrannical and backward state that wanted to forever extinguish the light and the democracy that was born of Greek culture and civilization. The great tragedian thus foretold the future oppression the Balkans underwent at the hands of the Ottoman Empire.

Aeschylus's greatness was not born out of the solitude of the writer's study—it emerged from the noisy communal mumblings. At a time when the *The Persians* was being staged, the Persian Empire had already been beaten in two different battles, but its threatening aura still loomed over Greece.

Did Aeschylus ever consider—in that blind, creative explosion of the mind where logic does not dare approach—that his tragedy might one day be played in a Persian capital, in the Persian language? One can hardly know. In our time, the desire to be translated into different languages is a common one for writers. But during Aeschylus's time, imagining your play on a Scythian or Persian stage would have been analogous to a modern-era writer envisioning his play being acted out on a celestial body, somewhere in outer space. If, however, Aeschylus did not consider the possibility of his play being one day played out on a Persian stage, how could we explain how little hatred the work reserved for the Persians?

In truth, by seeing the drama through the eyes of the Persians, Aeschylus recreated not only the darkness of an empire on the verge of catastrophe, but also the tragedy of a foreign people on whose shoulders fell the burden of an insane campaign of conquest.

But what is truly astonishing is the extreme sensibility that allowed Aeschylus to transcend his time and travel beyond the boundaries of Greece, which must have seemed the center of the world, to arrive at the darkness and barbarism of the Persian Empire. Transcendent, Aeschylus felt he was writing for all the people of the world, even if they still lived in barbarism, darkness, and sadness.

When we speak of *The Persians*, we must remember that aside from ideas that continue to be relevant, the play also exudes a fatalism of the time. For instance, according to Aeschylus and his contemporaries, the gods considered it acceptable for Eastern people and empires to fight on continental land. Destruction on land was acceptable, but destruction on sea was not. Crossing the sea was deemed punishable. The earthly empire of the Persians was lost the moment it transgressed on this limit set by the gods. In the description of the Battle of Salamis, in order to make it clear that the sea "does not fit with the barbarians," Aeschylus describes how ridiculous the attire of the sailors looked when their bodies floated on the waves of the Aegean.

The Persian campaign was an extraordinary betrayal of the gods. It was an official betrayal, or, more precisely, a doctrine masquerading as a betrayal. Who belongs on the sea and who belongs on the desert, who is born for the mountains and who is born for the rivers—these questions give rise to that tragic migration that came to be known as the separation of spheres of influence in the twentieth century. This separation began between the Assyrians and the Egyptians, the Greeks and the Romans, the Romans and the Byzantine. In our time, we have London, Paris, Washington, and Moscow.

The drama of the Persians contains messages that are just as important to the Greeks as they are to the Balkans at large. One of these was the call for unity against a common enemy. Infighting had been a lingering malaise in Ancient Greece. Let us remember *The Iliad*, which begins by chronicling an epidemic of infighting. The lack of communication between city-states, and in particular between Athens and Argos, was a perpetual burden for the tragedian. This was clear in *The Persians* and *The Oresteia*, and even more evident across the gates of Thebes.

The Thebaid must have been in circulation at a time when Greece experienced tremendous artistic development. The spiritual and artistic creative process that was occurring in Greece at the time resembled a high-density, celestial space. Pieces of ancient poems fragmented by time wandered around, ancient motifs either exploded with a bright light like new stars or aged and cooled off, new stars were born and old stars collided into one another. There was an endless process of disturbance and distortion, and an underlying, constant threat that a black hole would erupt into being, ready to absorb and destroy everything.

It is easy to lose track of the broad and diverse constellation of ancient Greek mythology and oral archaic poetry that came into being as different rhapsodies crashed into one another, expanded, or absorbed other songs. Only the minds and wills of geniuses like the Greek tragedians could have contained this debauchery and made it follow the standard parameters of drama. Without their interference, this diversifying mythology would have slowly collapsed—a fate that was suffered by Albanian oral epic poetry, which reached the twentieth century heavily and, in some cases, irreparably damaged.

The diversity of oral poetry contained both its own creation and dissolution. The titanic intervention of Homer and of the tragedians saved oral poetry from its own intoxicating debaucheries. Without that intervention, it would have been suffocated by its own diversity, or, in other words, by how it misunderstood its own freedom.

The Greek tragedians were the first to understand this danger. The limits of censorship and the hoaxes of the selection committee were naturally quite annoying, but an undetermined freedom, a wandering of everyone's mind according to its own desires, was perhaps even more fatal to art.

Aware of this danger, the Greek dramaturges created a barrier, a straitjacket that would limit their wayward freedom. This barrier was the law of unison among three elements: place, time, and subject matter. Much like taming a wild beast, they locked their divine madness within this frame of drama.

With the passage of centuries, as censorship and punishments for writers grew harsher, this self-immolation seemed more and more useless. It was William Shakespeare who threw aside the handcuffs, because by that point the tyrannical state had grown so repressive that it did not need help from the artists themselves. By then, the state had come to threaten writers with imprisonment, and, whenever necessary, with a real straitjacket.

The variety and freedom was inevitably passed on to the more cultivated literature. Although the majority of Greek tragedies are lost, in the remaining minority there are many overlaps between Aeschylus, Sophocles, and Euripides. Three different dramas centralize Orestes, a state of affairs that according to the Englishman H. C. Baldry, is the equivalent of having three different Macbeths written by three different geniuses.

Is it a good or a bad thing to have three different dramas about Orestes? Would it be a good or a bad thing to have three Macbeths?

The answer is not a simple one. Three Macbeths might be unnecessary—ten would undoubtedly be a catastrophe.

But let us return to the story at the doors of Thebes. As we know, the third part, which deals with the conflict between the two brothers, is the only part of the trilogy that has survived.

When the curtain opens, the public has no idea what happened between Eteocles and Polynices, or what made one of them flee from his fatherland. The agreement between the two brothers to rule Thebes by turns was broken by the brother currently in power, thus leading to the exile of the other. The whole story develops from the perspective of Eteocles, the defender of Thebes, and we have no sense of Polynices's perspective. His side of the story is not as convincing, given that he brought enemies of Thebes to her doors. Polynices sacrificed his fatherland for his ambition. Eteocles, even if he shares in his brother's guilt and ambition, assumes the heroic role of the fatherland's protector. Despite his darkness, he is without doubt one of the most pathetic figures in the whole of Greek literature.

There has been much speculation among scholars regarding the culpability of each brother. But perhaps despite the fact that one brother was painted as a hero and the other as a villain, both brothers were equally guilty. This thought was sustained by the figure of Antigone, their sister, who appears at the end of Aeschylus's tragedy and becomes the key protagonist in Sophocles's *Antigone*, the curtain for which lifts just as that of *The Seven* drops.

This whole conversation is nonessential, and neither is explaining everything according to a mythical perspective that conceptualizes the oedipal drama as man's fight with fate. The mythical perspective places this fight against fate at the core of tragedy, so that the oedipal drama was the fulfillment of a divine curse aimed against a family that disobeyed divinity through parricide, incest, fratricide, and, to round out this morbid cycle, the burial of a living sister, Antigone.

Despite spending thousands of pages exploring the oedipal complex, many scholars have failed to delve into the reasons that might have compelled Aeschylus to write *The Seven Against Thebes*. This tragedy was not born of some deep interest on the part of the tragedian regarding the oedipal complex, but instead from the disturbance of the times. *The Seven Against Thebes* is a warning the great Aeschylus issued his contemporaries about political division and the dangers that came from the East.

During Aeschylus's time, the massive empire of the Persians grew near the boundaries of small Greece like a shadow. Although in comparison to Greece this state was backward and totalitarian, neither its backwardness nor its darkness prevented some Greek leaders from periodically asking for the help of their "barbarian" neighbors. Many Greek leaders, blinded by contempt for their own people, sought shelter with the Persians and began to march against their own country. Such was the case with the leaders of Boetia and Thessaly, or Hippias, who turned to the Persians when they were getting near Marathon. This is what Constantine P. Cavafy had in mind when he wrote about the glory of those who fell in Thermopylae:

And even more honor is due to them
when they foresee (as many do foresee)
that in the end Ephialtis will make his appearance,
that the Medes will break through after all

The universality of *The Seven* was verified many times over. These deserting Greek princes reincarnated centuries later in the defecting Balkan princes of Greek, Albanian, and Slavic origin. Due to infighting, they were tempted by the Ottoman Empire in the same way that Greek princes were tempted by the Persians. They began to ask for the Ottomans' help to battle one another.

The Ottomans bestowed their favors willingly, so long as the Balkan princes gave up something in return. At first, the princes provided declarations and promises that they thoughtlessly believed they would not have to keep. Then, they renounced their names and religion. The Albanian counts and barons were especially renowned for this particular kind of insanity. George, John, and Paul turned their names into Mehmet and Ali, and replaced the titles "count" and "duke" with "pasha" and "vizier" as though this were all a game. This game would bring them down eventually.

On the eve of the Ottoman attack on the Balkans, the peninsula was still dotted by countless ancient amphitheaters left behind from the past. A drama played out in them might have woken up the mad princes. But the theatrical railings had long since gathered rust. The drama that was not played out in them was experienced in 770 city doors where the blood flowed without end. This horror was a punishment brought about by the Balkans' unwillingness to listen to omens and messages issued not by the gods, but by a dramaturge from antiquity.

Like every work of art, *The Seven Against Thebes* cannot be condensed into a single idea, no matter how powerful that idea might be. The work contains many mysterious moments of internal brilliance that take much work to explore in full. When the seven houses confront each other, for example, it is as though their leaders were a mirror that reflected and replicated evil. They often participate in conflict against one another as though in a dream, foretelling real wounds through painted wounds. The technique of building a dream with a revelatory ending is commonly used in Greek theater. Divine omens and foreboding signs circle around the dream repeatedly. The Ottoman threat is the natural, revelatory ending to a warning that was first issued two thousand years ago by Aeschylus.

In the description of Christmas in a small Albanian village, after celebratory fires, dances, and candles, Jeronim de Rada goes into a brilliant digression:

> In the sky
> The angels made their own banquet.

The divine space is as significant in Balkan poetry as it was in antiquity. The unique merit of the tragedians is that, just like Homer, they never abused this space. Otherwise, caught up in the boundlessness and timelessness of this space, they would have gotten lost in all its freedom.

The divine space was never a mere shelter where one could rest from life's struggles. The fact that this kingdom, Mount Olympus, was always visualized on Earth and bound to the shadowy, underground realm, suggests that the gravitational pull of art remained Earth-bound.

The refusal to be seduced by the celestial realm is captured by the drama of Prometheus, a work whose titanic dimensions are unprecedented. The battle that the spectator views on the scene is dizzying in its size and majesty. It is not a struggle between two groups, and neither does it deal with some shared curse rooted in a misfortune of the time. Nor does *Prometheus* deal with the confrontation of crime and conscience. In *Prometheus*, we have dimensions that are even more universal—we see divinities clash over the fate of the entire human race.

In an enormous canvas where a seemingly eternal stretch of drama unfolds between immortal characters, Prometheus is fittingly titanic. Colossal in size, yes, but titanic, first and foremost, internally. The drama's conflict is similarly colossal—it deals with the effacement and replacement of civilization. The conflict is born over the loss of something irretrievable.

This threat to civilization underlies the daily struggles, the passions, and the clashes separating human groups. It is an anxiety that we, the inhabitants of the human planet in the second half of the twentieth century, all share—namely the fear that we shall destroy humanity in a nuclear catastrophe.

And if the Ancient Greeks could have imagined the end of the world (imaginings that grew more frequent due to different religions in the Middle Ages), this end would have seemed secondary to their vision of hell, which they experienced as though it were the basement of their house.

In truth, *Prometheus* is not about the disappearance of civilization, but rather about its replacement. This does not diminish the anxiety it engenders. Instead, it makes it more majestic. The disappearance of civilization has been a source of anxiety for mankind for twenty-five centuries, and this fear only became more tangible in the twentieth century. The replacement of humanity (the process of othering the human face, or, in other words, of dehumanizing it), is a danger that has been present since ancient times and that will always exist.

In an interesting coincidence, Aeschylus and other writers fore-told this self-effacement of civilization in their art. Pulling human-ity from the roots in order to replace it with another humanity has been the fantasy of tyrants since the time of Aeschylus. With the passage of time, as crueler centuries arrived, this became the prized dream of the darkest dictators known to man. How often in their nights of delirium, frustrated with the people they commanded, did they dream, and perhaps even strategize, about creating a dejected people to populate a nightmare that only their twisted brains could engender?

Aeschylus's desire to preserve humanity, whose weaknesses he knew better than anyone and yet still managed to love, was one of the most timeless omens of his work. This anxiety determines the internal, titanic nature of *Prometheus*.

We do not know what existence Zeus had imagined in lieu of the life known to humankind; we just know that it would have been a lesser one. Other divinities heard Zeus's imaginings indifferently. Only Prometheus, who possessed the power of premonition and could sense the impending danger, pitied the humans. He rebelled against Zeus, fully aware that this was a self-sacrificial act, which only rendered his revolt more sublime.

With the passage of millennia, the figure of Prometheus, whom Marx understands as the first sacred martyr of the philosophical calendar, grew more heroic. From era to era, instead of becoming dimmer, he grew brighter and got closer to the people.

Prometheus was condemned for stealing the eternal fire, but we know that this was merely another crime in a string of offenses com-mitted to protect the humans. In fact, these other crimes constitute the majority of the case against Prometheus. As it often happens in courts of law, one particular action is emphasized, even though there were other, weightier actions to consider.

It is well-known that Prometheus, who pitied the human race and wanted to save it from death, shared with it fire and skills like sane judgment, memory, writing, and even treating the ill. Prometheus is a perpetual symbol of progress, civilization, rebellious martyrdom, and creativity. However strange it may seem, he is both an innovator and a conserver: an innovator because he opened new horizons for humanity, and a conserver because he preserved the race from extinction. He is a challenger of the gods, an indefatigable thousand-year-old martyr. Not only was he not afraid of Zeus, he dared call him a tyrant, and even predicted the supreme god's eventual downfall. For all this, Prometheus was struck by Zeus's lightning and thrown into an abyss. Zeus eventually freed Prometheus as a reward for not revealing the secret knowledge that could have led to Zeus's downfall. How often have tyrants descended into the holes where they keep their opponents in order to discover some secret, which was usually a concoction of their own sick minds?

We are nearing the end of Prometheus's tragedy as we know it. When the curtain falls, we leave the titan buried under a mountain of stone and rocks, where he will spend thousands and thousands of years. Unlike the spectators of antiquity, who only took a small break to eat or drink something they had brought before continuing to watch the rest of the drama, we can leave the theater. The ancient viewer's passion far outweighed our own; they saw two parts of the trilogy that we have not seen, nor will we ever be able to see.

The two thousand spectators who witnessed the full *Prometheus* are long dead. Two parts of Prometheus's tragedy died alongside them. The possibility provided by Einstein to capture the images of the past through some kind of movement in spaces where those images have not arrived yet is entirely theoretical. No matter how much we may advance, it is naive to think that a camera placed somewhere in space, waiting for the arrival of old images of what transpired in our planet, could capture, even faintly, a staging of *Prometheus* that hailed from a bygone millennium.

This is merely a fantasy, and we are obliged to accept the irretrievable loss.

We can console ourselves ever so slightly by reminding ourselves that we know something about the content of the lost trilogy. In *Prometheus Unbound*, after the long stay underground, the titan finally emerges and is forgiven by Zeus—no one knows why. We know only that in the third part of the trilogy Prometheus resumes his lost place in Olympus. He is also rewarded by Zeus for his thousand-year-long sufferings by being declared the god of artisanal works and ceramics, by being honored through traditional parties full of fire breathers (fire, which dealt most of his suffering), and by being presented with a ceramic crown in memory of the handcuffs of his martyrdom.

A series of inevitable questions arise from this information. Is there a contradiction at the titan's core between his early stance, when he disdains Zeus's forgiveness, and his later acceptance of Zeus's favors? Who caved first, Prometheus or Zeus? In short, was this a de-heroization or a hyper-martyrdom?

One might wonder if humanity lost the tragedies in order to avoid these difficult questions.

The key to the problem cannot be found within Aeschylian tragedy, but outside of it, in the criticism that for centuries thousands have directed at the fire-bringing titan. Perhaps, then, this drama was the product of a co-authorship between Aeschylus and humankind. The Prometheus that Aeschylus extracted from the common myths was enriched by hundreds of generations with endless, nameless personal dramas, and thus it arrived in its new incarnation to the present time.

Naturally, a silent friction between the tragedian and humanity where the figure of Prometheus is concerned exists. Humanity was doubtlessly in the right, but, nonetheless, it would be unfair to blame the tragedian for his lapse in objectivity.

Prometheus's trilogy, regardless of the genial and far-reaching mind of Aeschylus, is a product of its time. The gaze of the genius often transcended his period, but at times it was bound to fall within its boundaries. According to the ancient Greeks, irrevocable and longstanding enmities were unpardonable. We should not forget that we are dealing with a genre whose public was directly affected by these sorts of popular preconceptions. The unnecessary conflict between two Olympic divinities would have been incomprehensible to the Greek spectator. Although it is unclear how this was resolved, one thing is definite: Zeus gained little from the thousand-year-old conflict, except perhaps for a stroke to his ego or information regarding his eventual downfall. Prometheus, on the other hand, stood to gain his freedom and more. He saved the human race from extinction, was declared the god of work and art, and his face and crown were eternally preserved in the ancient ceramic. According to the ancient Greeks, these favorable conditions made his reconciliation with Zeus a dignified and reasonable one, and it is safe to assume that in the next two parts of the tragedy, the fury against Zeus's brutality might have abated somewhat.

Aeschylus's creative courage has Promethean dimensions. *Prometheus Bound* is the only Greek tragedy in which Zeus is depicted negatively. Zeus not only confronts Prometheus as a cruel tyrant, but we see how the son of Cronos paved his path with violent and unprecedented crimes, such as, like many other power-hungry, parricidal divinities, the act of overthrowing his own father from power.

This seems to evince Aeschylus's majestic idea that his contemporaries' divinities, including Zeus himself, have been through a long process of fine-tuning that normalized and made them more palatable.

But were the autocrats of Aeschylus's time similarly softened? Might ancient Greek tragedies, by depicting divinities not realistically, but according to how they should be, help temper the autocrats of their time? History has shown that not to be the case. In fact, over the course of centuries, the world came to know increasingly harsh rulers in whose palaces occurred crimes even more horrific than those of King Oedipus.

Does this mean that Aeschylus's art, with its foreboding and omens, went to waste? Of course not.

Aeschylus reminds us all, but especially world leaders, that autocrats and even gods are redeemable. If divinities and tyrants do not redeem themselves, then all the worse for them. Aeschylus's call that they become more civilized was not wasted, for it reminded people that their leaders are not who they should be, and thus awakened necessary revolts.

Even after Aeschylus had issued his warning to autocrats in the form of Prometheus, tyrannical cruelty did not soften. But this should not make us forget that the great tragedian was the first to rise to the challenge and create prometheanism, without which the world would be flatter and paler.

"At the end of the scene, the palace of Atreus." These are the stage directions that commenced the monumental *The Oresteia*, the only drama to have emerged from the Aeschylian oblivion in complete form. This note may have been the author's or a later stage director's—it doesn't matter. In front of us is a palace with three doors, under which occurred some of the most tragic events that the human mind can imagine. Through one door entered King Agamemnon, who was never to walk on the palace's purple carpet again. Through the other came out Queen Clytemnestra with her bloody axe, looking to justify what she had just done. Through the last of these doors, their son, Orestes, exited a matricide. He held the cloak with his father's dried blood in his hands. Orestes legitimized his murder in front of the world, but the Erinyes came to darken his eyes and turn his speech into senseless babble.

These horrors are merely the grandchildren of old crimes that for years had brewed inside the palace. These walls had already heard frightening things: murders between power-hungry brothers, a macabre banquet where the guests were fed the limbs of their living children, nightmares of disturbed consciences, curses, and anxieties.

Aeschylus derived the motivations for this horror from the old eposes that talked of the curse weighing on the palace of Atreus, where family blood vengeance, bound with the struggle for power, generated one murder after another. Aeschylus's idea that crime begets crime is underlined in this work more clearly than anywhere else, and anti-tyrannical ideas dominate the trilogy from beginning to end. News of a murder in this palace soon turns into anxiety—might this mean the rise of a new tyrant? When Agamemnon's death is exposed, the quick and disordered ancient choir resembles a group of contemporary journalists at the doors of a presidential building where there has been a coup d'état.

One of the main motifs of the work is the question of whether the maternal or paternal blood is the dominant one, an issue that has caused endless conflict on Earth and has been the foundation of many an old juridical code.

The Oresteia advances this subject clearly. The old divinities, the Erinyes, suggest that the bloodline comes from the mother. The newer gods, such as Athena and Apollo, suggest that it comes from the father. Friedrich Engels suggests that this was a distant echo of the millennial tension between the matriarchy, which was losing ground, and the emerging patriarchy. This reverberation would have been too old to draw Aeschylus if it had not generated new ideas regarding the Athenian court, whose power had become a point of contention between Athens and Argos.

The questions of justness that cuts across the entirety of Aeschylus's work is treated in *The Oresteia* as a confrontation between the Erinyes's understanding of justice and the new sense of justice being propagated by the state mechanism.

Like all great artistic works, *The Oresteia* defies every scheme of judgment. It is a drama of crimes and vengeance, of the anxieties of war for power, of the confrontation and the downfall of law, of foggy dreams and of omens. As such, *The Oresteia* is both general and specific, with temporal and spatial extensions that are even broader than those of *The Iliad* and *The Odyssey*.

The trilogy begins with the sacking of Troy, but gradually the entire history of this war unfolds majestically. We learn about the fatal night that began, according to the Greek memory, with the misfortune of Troy. Toward dawn on that night, Helen says:

> [I]f only death had pleased me then, grim death,
> that day I followed your son to Troy, forsaking
> my marriage bed, my kinsmen and my child,
> my favorite, now full grown . . .

In spare verses of rare beauty, we learn of the sadness that fell over the palace after the queen left, of the despair of her abandoned husband, Menelaus, and of the gathering of the Greek soldiers in Aulides, where Agamemnon, the head commander, sacrificed his daughter. A dark grief befell Greece as bad news and coffins kept arriving from Troy. The Greeks had overreached and would shoulder this ethical weight on their conscience for centuries.

In short, *The Oresteia* was a complete encyclopedia of the first world war, where tens of states and thousands of peoples were in conflict with one another like never before. Only in brief reminiscences and within a drama about something else entirely did the tragedian refer to this great campaign. In each of these brief interventions unfold huge vistas and thoughts.

Aeschylus testifies, for example, on the staid winds that prevented the Greek fleets from departing, and on how Agamemnon took Calchas's advice and killed his daughter in order to reawaken the winds. Today's reader will try to uncover a great truth within this mythical fog. What winds kept the Greek fleet at bay, who was Calchas, and why did Agamemnon accept the sacrifice?

Researchers have answered some, but not all, of these questions. Calchas, for instance, is one of the most mysterious figures in the entirety of ancient literature. He is so nebulous that Shakespeare suggests the seer is none other than an undercover Trojan sent by Priam to delay the departing fleet, but who, in the process, became a double agent and a true Greek. Was his advice given in order to divide and disturb the Greeks, who had finally managed to come together in Aulides? It must be historically true that the Greek fleet did not depart toward Troy right away, but perhaps all of this discussion on winds truly indicated divisions within the Greek army—unstable alliances and the anxiety evoked by Troy. According to the information provided by ancient authors, if the Trojan War lasted ten years, gathering the Greek army also took about ten years. The advice of Calchas could have been delivered according to instructions by his master, Priam, or in defiance of these orders if Calchas was truly denying the old allegiance. The more likely explanation is that Calchas never delivered any advice, and that Iphigenia was sacrificed coldly, for purely political reasons. Agamemnon sacrificed his daughter not only due to his ambition, but also in order to legitimize his request that others sacrifice themselves in battle. Sovereigns have often done similar things before.

The speculation surrounding Iphigenia's sacrifice is heightened by Greek mythology and by the stories in which Artemis replaced the girl with a deer. These accounts support our own: this was a false sacrifice and a political performance.

The depression that envelops Troy reads like the plight of every family who sends their loved ones to battle only to get a coffin in return.

A bit further in the tragedy, the whirling of popular whispers against war suggest that instead of a husband, the wife receives a coffin. But there is worse still:

> The rampart's down, there, the great wall we trusted,
> our impregnable shield for the ships and men themselves.
> The enemy storms down on the rolling hulls nonstop . . .

This collective psychosis about a faraway war reminds us of the international burdens of our century created by the Korean, Vietnam, and most recently, the Afghanistan Wars. We know about the Trojan war through Homer, but thanks to Aeschylus, the story of Troy belongs to the twentieth century more than it does to any other time. In *The Persians*, Aeschylus sees Greece from afar, like an enemy would. In *The Oresteia*, the descriptions of Troy's fatal night, the barbaric massacre, and the outcries of those defeated in battle all exude incredible pain, as though they were witnessed through Trojan eyes.

These events are followed by the return of the Greeks to their homeland. The Greeks, who overstepped themselves in their thirst for vengeance, now suffer toilsome nights burdened by pangs of conscience. The time eventually came when the victors fell upon one another with blood axes. One of their palaces, that of Agamemnon, came to know three calamities, each more frightful than the next.

This is *The Oresteia*, a crown full of precious stones, each of which has the value of a small *Iliad* and the capacity, in its splendor, to capture all the fires and tragedy of Troy. There are other precious stones in the crown, but the red ruby at its center always shines the brightest. This ruby is the motif of blood vengeance; a motif that is particularly familiar to the people of the Balkans.

One uneventful afternoon, you find a book that might serve as a fitting companion to your reading of Aeschylus's texts. At times, you interrupt your reading of *The Oresteia* in order to leaf through this strange book just like you might look through a dictionary of ancient Greek.

52. No one may hinder anyone's passage on the village road and on the highway, even if these passageways are in front of one's own house. Where a man passes, livestock also walks. The living pass there and the dead are transported there. Even if the highway is ruined, muddy, or choked, all must travel on it—the wayfarer, the livestock, the bride with the bridegroom's men, and those who accompany the dead.

57. If a woman kills her husband and is then killed by her brother-in-law, this latter act is not permitted by the *Kanun*. The blood of a woman in not equal to the blood of a man. The father of the wife incurs his son-in-law's blood.

61. The wife does not have rights over her husband's children or house.

243. According to the *Kanun*, boundary stones and the bones of the dead are equal. To move a boundary is to move the bones of the dead.

602. The house of an Albanian belongs to God and to the guest.

620. If a guest enters your house, even though he may be in blood with you, you must say to him, "Welcome!"

649. In the *Kanun*, one can forgive the murdered father, brother, and relative; but one cannot forgive the murdered guest.

695. For the Albanian of the mountains, the chain of relationships of blood and kinship are endless.

699. Degrees of relationship by blood result are patriarchal; degrees of relationship by kinship are matriarchal.

700. Relationships stemming from the side of the father are called "The Tree of Blood."

701. Relationships stemming from the side of the mother are called "The Tree of Milk."

887. The value of all men's life is the same, whether a man is handsome or ugly.

888. Everyone considers himself good and says to himself, "I am an honorable man," when greeted with the phrase, "Are you an honorable man?"

901. If two men kill each other in the course of an argument, "a head for a death or blood for blood" has been lawfully fulfilled, since both are dead.

903. If one is killed and the other wounded, then the wounded man must pay the balance of the blood-money for the murdered man.

917. Blood is never unavenged.

1238. It is the custom to lament three times over the deceased, repeating the words, "Woe is me!" nine times.

1251. The friends who have scratched their faces to lament the dead must not wash off their blood either in the house or in the village of the deceased, but must wait until they arrive at their own homes.

1252. Mourning the death of a man in the family must last one year.

What constitution do these strange articles belong to? Are they the fruit of some fantasy?

These are only 19 of the 1,263 articles that form the Albanian law code known as the *Kanun*.

When these articles were gathered in writing by Shtjefën Gjeçovi, the code was still in operation. As though to close a fatal cycle, on October 14, 1919, at three in the afternoon, Gjeçovi himself was murdered in a manner similar to that noted in the ancient code.

This cruel, uniform code, transmitted orally from generation to generation throughout many centuries, envelops all of human life and death, carefully determining everything from how coffee is made to the rules for serving it. Violating these rules could lead to mortal enmities. An entire region could even be burned by way of punishment.

The *Kanun* is a whole encyclopedia of majesty and insanity, as tragic as it is grotesque.

The bells of livestock, the barking of shepherd dogs, windmills, gatherings of men, hunts, and wedding ceremonies were all inter-rupted by the brutal invasion of evil, murder, horrors, abductions of women, offenses at the dining table, illegality, violation of hos-pitality, blood vengeance from generation to generation, a funerary ceremony, and so forth.

The entire nation was caught up on the idea of justice, on the horror and disgust over blood, on incest, and on chaos. These fatalities, which hovered over everything like a cold and inescap-able sun, are not unlike that of the old tragedies. It is difficult to find people whose lives resembled the Greek theater more closely than the Albanians.

For years, ancient Greek literature has been said to have benefited from a range of artistic springs that grew in the territory sur-rounding Greece, such as the Assyrian, Babylonian, and Egyptian myths, ancient poems like *The Epic of Gilgamesh*, and the oral traditions of its Balkan neighbors. These sources generously grant the Greek metropolis treasures to add to its colossal spiritual wealth in the form of myths, droplets of oral poetry, the strangest artistic imaginings, and the names of divinities that were making their way toward the Greek universe and supplanting regional deities.

Among the endless ranks of studies about ancient Greek litera-ture, there are not enough analyses that connect its roots and omens with the bedrock of the collective Balkan experience, the ancient Greeks' closest and oldest neighbors.

Certain circumstances have contributed to this reality. One of the key reasons has been, undoubtedly, the Roman path through which Greek literature passed into the European heritage. It was the Romans who, after allowing themselves to be completely overwhelmed by the power of Greek literature, published, republished, and fully dissected it. Greek literature became known to the rest of the world alongside this Roman commentary.

This is also where the first tampering with Greek literature by the Romans began. Despite the high esteem in which the Romans held Greek art, it cannot be forgotten that they were invaders of the harshest kind. As such, they could not understand the deep wells from which emerge the omens of a people, those that guide and determine its art. Proud and dismissive toward those they had conquered, the Romans were ill-prepared to understand the influence that the Balkan people had on one another, particularly when it came to exchanging their spiritual treasures. Sadly, the Romans' perfunctory gestures, long explorations, and Latin theses about ancient Greek literature all assumed an official tone in the European world and are still considered authoritative texts, even centuries after the fall of the Roman Empire.

The development of European countries and the stagnated progress of the Balkan nations made many forget the land that at one point had given birth to ancient miracles. Despite the calls of Byron, Shelley, Goethe, and Hölderlin, European countries inherited the Romans' dismissal of the Balkans, to whom they owed the roots of their civilization.

This indifference toward the fate of the Balkan people indicates that other countries considered Greek art and literature a universal treasure lacking a proper home. The tragic backwardness of the Balkan people meant that their participation in the world conversation about antiquity was meager. The owners of the house were thus sidestepped for a very long time.

In the nineteenth century, after Greek independence, and later on, after the liberation of other Balkan countries from the Ottoman occupation, Balkan voices were heard again. Albanian dignitaries, for instance, wrote and spoke about the connections between Greek art and the Albanians. Famous scholars from other countries, like Hahn, Lambertz, Jokk, and Gosemann, not only began to accept the inevitability of this connection, but also helped us understand it better. This comparative research continues still. For instance, Jean-Pierre Vernant and Pierre Vidal-Naquet recreated in French, under the title *A Romanian Oedipus*, an old Romanian ballad, also collected and published in 1967 by the Romanians themselves. The similarity that Vernant and Vidal-Naquet find between the Greek myth of Oedipus and the Romanian ballad is entirely visible, and it is regrettable that such studies are all too infrequent. In truth, there are tens of old Balkan songs where we find echoes of the myth of Oedipus and of other ancient myths. These echoes are particularly clear in ballads about military and economic migration.

These necessary migrations heavily burdened the Balkan people. Military service, which could take place anywhere in the Ottoman Empire, including distant regions like the deserts of Yemen or Saudi Arabia, assumed hellish dimensions. A large part of the recruits never returned, or came back altered from the long time spent in service or under the desert sun. Heart-wrenching ballads captured the plight of these characters.

The economic exile that began after the liberation of the Balkans from the Ottoman Empire had similar geographical dimensions, except that now America, Australia, and other faraway places stood in for the distant Arabian lands. Many who left their land due to economic hardships returned either transformed or not at all.

In order to articulate the pain of these two forms of exile, the people of the Balkans dug into their collective creative consciousness and dredged up old models, the same artistic mechanisms that had earlier created the songs of absence and return. The shadows of Odysseus, Agamemnon, and Oedipus lurked behind the military recruiters or the immigrants headed for the United States. Neither the military service in the desert nor the lights of Brooklyn and Manhattan erased the ancient disturbance from their conscience. In fact, when they sang of these new dramas they supplanted Arabian and American vistas with the formula that had been used to cook the old poems and the tragic theater. So, unsatisfied with the ballads that recounted the economic difficulties of the soldier whose family relied on him, the popular muse sought universal dimensions for this new drama. It sought a marriage outside the family.

Since the earlier Middle Ages, the Balkans had treated the theme of the soldier who had been supposed dead and, upon his return, accidentally married his sister. *Oedipus* develops as a reversal of the economic migrant who returns to Albania from the United States. In *Oedipus*, it is not the son but the father who migrates for a long time, and, upon his return, is killed by his son. In the case of the incestuous siblings, Balkan ballads interrupted this transgression at the last minute with excuses, memories, and signs. Deep misunderstanding occurs in the story about the return of the émigré who kills his own son. This is the reason why scholars consider their endings optimistic. I think the endings, optimistic or not, do not change anything about the value of these songs, and the standing of the popular muse resembles Sophocles, who says that everyone has dreamed of sleeping with their mothers.

Naturally, much of the relationship between the works of the ancient tragedians and their later Balkan echoes remains undiscovered. Albanian epic poetry, one of the oldest forms of literature in the peninsula, has a depth of unplumbed reflections that deal with the old mythology.

This poetic closeness is not accidental. The Albanians, despite having a language that was fundamentally different from that of the Greeks, were nonetheless similar to them in many other ways. Recently, Jacques Lacarrière, while discussing an independent Greece, wrote: "This face is not always tangible, but as we have seen, an independent Greece, reborn again, and nonetheless authentically Greek, was still covered under the Turkish, Albanian, and later Bavarian flourishing. This was undoubtedly one of the unique characteristics of this new state: it was born and raised under different masks, foreign and derived from her captors or saviors."

We must ask, then: if the Turkish mask was the captor's and the German mask the savior's, whose was the Albanian mask? The answer is simple: the Albanians were merely the perpetual neighbors of the Greeks, and any similarity between the two was the result of this neighborly coexistence, which could be traced back across the depth of centuries.

All one needs to do is turn to nymphs and divinities like Circe, the Erinyes, Cyclops, and Orestes, who all appear frequently in ancient Albanian poetry, in order to discover the Greek names and phenomena that can only be explained through the Albanian language. Albanian poetry, then, is not a mere echo left behind by the great tragedians—it is the shared cultural bedrock between the Illyrians and the Greeks. *The Oresteia*, the fullest and most beautiful testimony of ancient tragedy, is the most convincing proof of this.

Blood vengeance is a common phenomenon in many parts of the world, but vengeance among the Balkans, and particularly among the Albanians, is remarkably entrenched in the governing mechanism that regulates the entire juridical, moral, and philosophical life.

As a universal phenomenon of mankind, blood vengeance, however dark its name and essence, has also been one of the first elements of juridical culture. The French Homeric scholar Pierre Carlier makes a great rediscovery when he writes that the first poetic text in the world dealt with a juridical motif related to blood vengeance.

In 1999, 2,500 years after the famous poem was first written, Carlier began to question the adequacy of the hundreds of translations that *The Iliad* had inspired. His questions arose because a trial seemed much too simple to belong alongside the foundational images of the world constructed by Ephesus.

In truth, not only does the trial seem much too simple, but if you examine the matter more closely, it also seems that there was little reason to hold such a trial in the first place. Neither was there a reason for as large a group of people to be torn apart from tempestuousness and passion.

Carlier came to the conclusion that there is something occluded in the Ancient Greek text. Homer did not feel the need to explain things to his contemporaries, who were likely familiar with great legal judgments. The text thus appears nebulous for people of other times, who, unable to find what lay behind these hazy passages, have chosen the path of least resistance by reducing the text of the trial to a question of punishment or absolution.

Carlier manages to uncover the enigma. An experienced reader of Homer and Greek, he brings out the hidden meaning of the text.

The issue is not simply about a murder, but rather refers to a classic question of blood vengeance. According to Carlier's interpretations, one of the aggrieved parties demands the repayment of the blood debt, while the victim's clan does not accept the repayment and expects the continuation of the blood vengeance.

As the French scholar helps us realize, this is a legal case because we are in one of the foundational places of blood vengeance. We see a clash between two ancient currents: one demands to be freed from the norms and the other insists on the opposite.

This blood vengeance trial was considered by Homer worthy of being depicted alongside other foundational elements of life: the Earth, the ocean, the stars, cities celebrating, and people mourning.

Let us return to the Albanian mountains. Should the Albanians be embarrassed that in the twentieth century they continued to hold judgments of the blood like those of Homer's time? Naturally, this is nothing to be proud of. And yet, blood vengeance has always been central to the Albanian story.

Blood vengeance, which seems cruel and horrific, was one of the foundations of justice. Those foundations are always murky. At the base of the emancipation of humanity there is a dark and most vicious apparatus: hell. No human invention comes close to this machine. It makes people responsible for their actions through the anxiety and horror it inspires. It created the idea of punishment and therefore of justice, thus improving the human conscience.

Blood vengeance was one of the visible parts of the underground, hellish machine that extended its coldness and cast its heavy shadow over Earth. We should pity rather than judge the Albanians, who were tormented and disfigured by blood vengeance until so recently.

Let us return to Aeschylus's trilogy. *The Oresteia* has been the only ancient work of literature where the motifs of blood and judgment align so closely with the Albanian law code. The ancient text touched upon moments that are fundamental to the code, such as the violation of hospitality and the punishment that ensues from this transgression.

According to the code, the judges in these cases would go as far as to count the wounds on the victim's body in order to determine more precisely what repayment was due. This went even further: one of the main motifs in *The Oresteia* is the infighting between divinities, much like the Athenian judges argued over of the dominance of either maternal or paternal blood. This old argument has been repeated thousands of times in the judgments of blood near the stone towers of the Albanian mountain-dwellers. The Albanian law code was shaped, just like *The Oresteia*, upon murder.

As to the conflict between the maternal and paternal lineage, this question is usually played out in terms of property. In the code, however, just like in *The Oresteia*, this conflict is unrelated to property, and is instead negotiated by the order in which blood-vengeance is claimed.

It is interesting to underline that this similarity does not occur in those parts of Albania that are closest to Greece, but instead in the Albanian Northern Alps, which were cold and dark places that the ancient Greeks might have conjured when they imagined the wasteland where Prometheus was banished.

The similarities do not stop there: this tragedy, like the *Kanun*, raises the question of whether humankind should be restrained by the system of blood or by the mechanism of the state.

The ancient Greeks lost their own code, which once resembled that of their neighbors, the Albanians. The Albanians preserved their code until recently, which is neither meritorious nor a sign of backwardness. The phenomenon endured due to a series of historical and geographical factors, such as the nature of the occupation in some areas of the Balkans and the tenuous independence that was being preserved in other areas, particularly in the mountains.

In comparison to Roman law, the Albanian code was rudimentary, but the Albanians liked that it placed public opinion above all else. Engels argues that familial codes can only be enforced by public opinion—hence their fundamental conflict with power. The last thing that the Romans cared about was the public opinion of the people they subjugated.

The Albanian code invited further Roman animosity for another reason: there is an ominous absence in a code so detailed that it outlines even the minutia of acceptable greeting expressions: the laws that regulate an occupier are as absent as a ghost in the *Kanun*.

A thousand years later, when Greece had been buried in the Byzantine sunset, the Albanian counts and princes were on the verge of a renaissance. But just as the Albanians were ready to discard the old code, the Ottoman eclipse overwhelmed the Greeks, the Albanians, and all of the art of their beautiful peninsula. When confronted with Turkish law, the Albanians merely returned to their thousand-year-old *Kanun*, just as it was, bloody but dignified in its tragic spirit. In five centuries of occupation and coexistence, the stubbornness of the Albanian *Kanun* withstood all tests. It was now the constitution not only of the Albanian Catholics, but also of those who converted to Islam. No modifications were made to it. It was as though Christianity still reigned in Albania like before.

But let us return to *The Oresteia*. The similarities between this tragedy and the Albanian *Kanun* date as far back as the Trojan war. Thousands of academic texts advance the theory that, although there were motivating economic factors, what fueled the Trojan conflict was the abduction of the beautiful Helen by the Trojan prince, Paris. The statement is fairly accurate, but greatly deficient nonetheless.

The mere abduction of a woman could not have awakened the murderous anger of people and divinities throughout Greece. Accounts of elopements and infidelities are countless in life and literature, but Helen's contained something unique.

Her abduction was not, as is commonly assumed, extraordinary because she was a queen. The Greeks understood a queen's role very differently: Helen was merely their leader's wife. She was not even the queen of Greece in its entirety—her husband ruled over the city-state of Sparta, making her one among tens of Greek "queens." Even if Helen's elopement had awoken an armed campaign and unified the other "kings," it would have caused their respective wives to oppose a battle being waged for their beautiful rival's sake.

It is likely that in the decade-long war preparations, some of the Greeks forgot what they were fighting over. It is also likely that they felt the need to substantiate the narrative of Helen's elopement with further injustices.

Aeschylus writes:

> Thus did the sinner Paris
> Come to the House of Atreus,
> Leaving the table spread for him
> Shamed with theft of a woman.

And further:

> O Zeus Almighty, O bountiful Night,
> Housekeeper of heaven's embroidery, thou
> Hast entangled the towers of the city of Troy
> In a fine-spun net, which none could escape,
> Not a man nor a child, nay all are entrapped
> In the far-flung coils of destruction.
> Great Zeus the Hospitable, him do I praise,
> Who hath punished at last the transgressor; for long
> Was his bow outstretched with unerring intent,
> That the shaft might not fall short nor escape
> Far out in the starry expanses.

The real misfortune here is not the elopement, but the violation of hospitality codes.

Prohibitions against "breaking the word," "betraying the guest," and "desecrating the table" are at the Albanian *Kanun*'s foundations, and transgressing these boundaries could lead not only to blood between families, but to enmity between whole regions.

The ritual of hospitality, just like that of blood vengeance, is not unique to the Balkans. However, the explanations of hospitality in the *Kanun* were so detailed they bordered on pedantic. This ritual and the violation of hospitality are even sung about in moving ballads. Even today, in distant mountainous areas, there are abandoned towers that to the Albanian eye seem hellish fortresses because they have housed a violation of the hospitality law.

Articles 1189 and 1190 in the *Kanun* delineate clearly what happens to a house where the guest is injured: "After burning the house, the remains of it are cut down, its stones are dislodged, and its four corners are razed to their foundations," which signifies that the house's "members have been banished forever from the area."

But all this adoration and care for the guest turned cold if he abused of his host's courtesy: "just as you are obliged to answer for an offense to your guest, so you are obliged to answer for an offense perpetrated by your guest." To the Albanian mountain-dweller, Macbeth and Paris are equally culpable—the former for laying a hand on his guest and the latter for violating his host's hospitality.

The *Kanun*'s hospitality code engendered the many Albanian tragedies covered avidly by newspapers in the 1920s and 1930s. To the Albanian mountain-dwellers, a stranger's request to spend the night was comparable to a request for political asylum, and it could result in armed conflict with whomever the stranger was in blood with. Many clans and villages got embroiled in such conflicts. Even the slightest traffic violation in Albania could turn into a violation of the code. During the times of the *Kanun*, the house was not the only place protected by the Albanian *besa*, or the sacred word— the streets in which one traveled were also blanketed by the code. Strangers walking a village's roads enjoyed the same safety that they did within the walls of the villagers' homes.

The broad implications of this particular besa have not been studied very thoroughly. It is not known, for instance, what a village stood to gain from ensuring strangers this protection. It is also not known whether roads on which the code was violated were subject to destruction like houses were. If a house was burned, what happened to the road that led up to it? Did they dig up big and irreparable holes or was it simply abandoned?

Independently of all this, what surfaces from the study of this phenomenon is the Albanians' tendency to replace the state apparatus with the *Kanun*. The validity of the besa in the public sphere testified to its expanding sphere of influence and growing dimensions. In this case, we can easily envision warfare between two villages, regions, or peoples over a safe road found on their border. (Part of the violence between the Serbs and the Albanians has classic roots in law codes like the *Kanun*.) So, if an Albanian mountain-dweller were to be told that centuries earlier a war had begun due to an elopement, he would look at you with surprise. But if you were to add that it was not merely an act of infidelity, but also an instance in which the oath of hospitality was broken, then this war, however bloody, would seem like the most natural thing in the world to him.

The modern-day Albanian's response is similar, if not identical, to that of the ancient people of the Balkans.

Judging by his insistence on the violation of hospitality as a core cause for the tensions between the Greeks and the Trojans, it appears as though Aeschylus was even more scrupulous than

Homer. But while the beginning of the campaign may have been dominated by this violation of hospitality, it is possible that during the Trojan siege Helen's romantic adventure emerged on the primary plane. This is understandable: a sinful, beautiful woman is more enticing than any moral code. Helen could more easily absorb the Greek soldiers' erotic fantasies, no doubt prolific after so many years away from women. Helen's infidelity likely provoked the soldiers' suspicion and anger as well, for if Helen left a king, what prevented their own wives from leaving them? As we sit here freezing, they seethed, our wives probably have another man in their warm bed. And so, in the soldiers' camps under the Trojan walls, Helen was declared the cause of the war.

According to the biochemist Kazuhiko Yamamoto, the *Kanun* may require that we consider its underlying influences in order to explore the depths of our theory regarding *The Oresteia*. Yamamoto proposes that we look to old Japanese rituals. According to the biochemist, these rituals are connected to the *Kanun* by the extremism of their hospitality laws. The Japanese scholar connects the Albanian *Kanun* with *marebito*, an ancient Japanese term that refers to a godly, masked being who visits villages and brings gifts of wisdom and happiness. Yamamoto suggests that imagining the stranger one agreed to host for the night as a god sustained the tragic Albanian code, according to which one can forgive the murder of a son, a brother, and even a father through a special ceremony, but never the spilled blood of a guest. Murdering a guest is equivalent to the violation of the deity, and only a bloody sacrifice can atone for it. The famous article in the *Kanun*, "The house of an Albanian belongs to God and to the guest," might be rephrased in the following way: "the house of the Albanian belongs to God and God" or, "the house of the Albanian belongs to God twice over."

Other such Aeschylian remnants can be found in our modern Balkan world, such as choral mourning, the habit of thumping on fresh burial grounds (according to the *Kanun*, this must be done so that the ground accepts the dead), or the Albanian linguistic construction of names ("Polynices," for example, would have been "the man who quarreled" in ancient Greek, and is "the man who slept much and was lucky" in contemporary Albanian). But instead of dwelling on all these things, let us focus on more important things.

Part two of the trilogy, *The Libation Bearers*, ends with Orestes's attempt to justify the murder he has just committed. After explaining to the chorus that he killed his mother to avenge the murder of his father, he shows the bloody netting that Clytemnestra threw over her husband before she stabbed him.

It seems odd that Clytemnestra saved this damning piece of evidence, and the manner in which she recounts what she has done is similarly strange and self-incriminating.

Orestes uses the bloodied fabric to incite popular hatred against the queen. He found the netting right away, which suggests that it had been kept visibly at hand.

Two difficult questions arise: first, why was the netting saved, and second, why was it kept in such a visible place?

If we justified this moment as a theatrical strategy, then a third, even harder question emerges: why was no one surprised, particularly the chorus, which helps move along the drama and reflects on everything? What is this netting? Why was it saved? Does it serve a perverse decorative function in the palace? One might, rightly, expect the chorus to voice such questions, but the chorus considered the bloody netting unremarkable, and so did Orestes. He is not enraged to see it hanging on the wall. He does not seem to have to look for it; in fact, he does not even have to ask his sister where it might be.

He simply knows where it is, much like a person knows the layout of their house and can find its fireplace and altar in the dark.

One can immediately sense that there was something here that Aeschylus's contemporaries knew and that we do not. The key to this can only be found far away, in the Albanian mountains. When someone is killed in the Albanian mountains, their blood shirt has to be hung from the killer's tower so that the bereaved family members can read the omens sent by the victim in the color of the drying blood. Through these blood shirts, which played an important role in the continuation of the *Kanun*, the family members learned whether the dead awaited the avenging of their blood with impatience, dismay, or hopelessness.

Clytemnestra carefully observes the bloodstains on the fabric with which she killed her husband, certain of Agamemnon's attempts to communicate with the living. She fears her husband's vengeance, suspects that Orestes is alive, and tries to read this connection between father and son in the blood. After murdering her husband, she attempts to interrupt this connection by cutting up the body of the victim in such a way that, according to the ancient Greeks, it can no longer send messages to Earth. Despite these measures, Clytemnestra is still vigilant. The importance of this zealously monitored blood is confirmed when Orestes and Electra stand over Agamemnon's grave and beg for his help. According to the Greeks, blood vengeance cannot be carried out properly without the help and approval of the dead.

Ideally, Clytemnestra would have preserved her husband's blood shirt. In the absence of a shirt, she saved the netting fabric.

The instant that Orestes walks into the palace, Clytemnestra despairs. Aeschylus tells us that her anxiety is rooted in a dream, but we know that he relied on different variants of the epos of the Atreus. In one variant, the fabric might have disturbed the conscience of the queen, just as the blood shirts hanging from towers in the Albanian mountains distressed the victims' relatives. It was not a dream, but a change in the color of the blood that frightened the queen.

Let us return to the butchering of Agamemnon's corpse.

In the prologue of part two of *The Oresteia*, when Electra incites Orestes's vengeance, the chorus implies that cutting up Agamemnon's body was as reprehensible as it was to kill him in the first place.

According to the choir, mutilating the body is not only macabre but also interrupts the cycle of blood vengeance. This violation of the communion between the dead and the living disrupts societal codes and is thus intolerable.

Having understood this, Orestes's outrage takes on a new dimension: it has societal value because it ensures the functioning of the code. Aeschylus does not tell us how the code is fed and preserved, but what he doesn't say has been made evident in the Albanian mountains for centuries.

Endless chronicles and ballads have dealt with the spiritual torture of young Albanian men wavering between blood vengeance and shame. Even though none of these men had ever heard Orestes's name, thousands of them reenacted his story in the mountains. "Land of Orestes" is perhaps a better name for the northern region of Albania than the current "Land of Eagles."

Blood vengeance in the northern Albanian mountains was horrible and widespread. It seemed as though all of life was arranged to the pace of signs, bells, and barometers that hurried blood avengers. A great, vigilant presence kept an eye on anything that could damage the *Kanun*, such as the hesitation of blood seekers or the crime of violating corpses. Not only was mutilating the corpse strictly forbidden, but the murderer even had to rearrange the victim's body so that it would lie in a dignified manner. There were also rules for what to do in case the murderer, overwhelmed by what had just happened, was unable to rearrange the body as needed.

> **846.** The murderer, if he is able to do so himself, will turn the victim over on his back. If he can, well and good: if not, he must tell the first person he meets to turn the victim over on his back and place his weapon on his head.

> **847.** The murderer may not take the victim's weapon. If he commits such a dishonorable act, he incurs two blood feuds.

Albanians despised Montenegrins for their habit of beheading enemies, something that the Slavs either learned from the Turks or brought from the remote steppes. The Albanians were so averse to tampering with corpses that their code excluded the use of a knife as a murder weapon, and mentions of cold weapons rarely crop up in Albanian ballads. Tussles were also deemed embarrassing, and therefore inadmissible.

Weapons that work from afar, like arrows and firearms, suited the *Kanun* best Albanians must have been dismayed when arrows were first replaced by swords and knives. But then a weapon appeared that seemed created especially for them: the rifle.

This aversion to mutilating the body is driven by a desire to protect the code. The logic was simple: tampering with the corpse broke kinship ties, thus endangering the continuity of the *Kanun*, and all measures were taken to ensure that nothing of the sort ever happened.

The Albanian code does not explain why it is so firmly set on preserving the corpse. Aeschylus provided the answer to this centuries earlier when he suggested that Orestes's shame is shot through with doubt—a dangerous duality that threatens to break down societal codes.

Other canonical habits of the Albanians are present in *The Oresteia* in either a sharp or a shadowy manner. Without the Albanian lens, it is hard to understand certain elements of the tragedy, such as Orestes's persistent knocking:

> Ho there, ho! Hear me, open to my knocking!
> O, who is there? Ho, who is at home?
> I call a third time for some answering step,
> If Aegisthus permits the house to grant
> Strangers their due of hospitality.

We feel the echo of the centuries-old cry of the *Kanun*: "Are you receiving guests, man of the house?"

The *Kanun* explains the boldness of Orestes, who, almost threateningly, knocks on a door that to him is nearly a stranger's, as though he were an Albanian traveler confidently demanding hospitality.

His boldness and aggression seem completely senseless without the *Kanun*—an aberration that is hard to envision in the work of a novice playwright, let alone in writings of the father of tragedy.

But here we have no illogical leap. Dissonance is avoided thanks to the codes of ancient Balkan hospitality. According to the *Kanun*, the door of every house, at every hour of the day and night, must be opened as soon as someone knocks and calls out "Are you receiving guests, man of the house?" Not only are these words binding, but the failure to heed their call is as strictly punished as any other crime.

603. The guest may not enter without calling out in the courtyard.

604. When the guest has called out, the master of the house or another resident must respond and lead him inside.

605. The guest is greeted, his weapon is taken, and he is brought into the house."

And, above all, the famous article:

620: If a guest enters your house, even though he may be in blood with you, you must say to him, "Welcome!"

This was the law that Orestes exploited in order to enter the house of Atreus.

More similarities are revealed by a careful investigation of the ancient Greek world as it appears in books, statues, and vases, and of the Balkan world in its living fullness. Even those who may not be in favor of researching this connective tissue must agree with great scholars and researchers who think that grounding the ancient Greeks "into concrete soil" might help deepen our understanding of their universe.

In the 1930s, American Homeric scholars Milman Parry and Albert Lord traveled to the northern Albanian and southern Yugoslavian regions—the last laboratories on Earth to produce Homeric epics. They resolved many questions about Homer by coming into contact with the singers of the time, whom they patiently surveyed to discover the secrets of their strange mastery.

Further study of oral poetry in the Balkans, now an abandoned creative site scattered with a few pearls of rare beauty, is a necessary if not indispensable endeavor. The value and radiance of these gems illuminate the depths of time and give answers to a host of questions that still haunt scholars.

From a careful reading of ancient literature, anyone can glean that the ancient Greeks were marble-like in their wisdom and serenity. They were, however, as wise as they were irrational, as logical as they were grotesque, and as aloof as they were impatient. Introverted and extroverted, resentful and heady, loyal and treacherous—they resemble the Balkan people, especially the Balkans of the turn of the nineteenth century, when the peninsula still retained a sense of cultural unity.

There is evidence everywhere that the human face of antiquity was less than idyllic. It is enough to recall the incident in which Euripides was forced to appear on the stage to calm an angry audience, explaining that what they demanded of his character would take place only a few moments later. The audience's great impatience gives us an apt idea of what the Athenian lovers of theater were like.

To confront such a crowd, the great tragedians had to have nerves of steel.

There was a period of time when modern Greeks suffered rather than gloried over their splendid lineage. They were like children being constantly reminded of their handsome, wise, and majestic parents. Swarthy, short, and mostly illiterate in the nineteenth century, they shattered the fantasies of lovers of antiquity. Until then, the modern Greeks had been dimmed by the Ottoman Empire. When they came to light, the disillusionment they prompted was so great that many wished they had remained under the cover of the Ottomans.

The Greeks were irritated by this disappointment to the point of wanting to destroy the insidious monuments to the past.

Their neighbors, the Albanians, although lighter in appearance and a bit taller, similarly despaired at the impossibility of rising to the height of their ancestors, the Illyrians. But while the Greeks invited the aggravation of others, the Albanians mainly brooded in isolation. "We are supposed to be the glorious Albanians"—they seemed to yell at the sight of one another after the emancipation. Where were the heroes of ballads and legends, the wise warriors, and the beautiful women?

But no matter how unlike their ancestors they were, these were the ancient Greeks' only grandchildren. With unmistakable intuition, the Albanians awoke in a world that looked to them strange and cold, and realized that in their orphaned state they had to embrace their forefathers even more closely. Lacking a larger tribe like the Slavs or the Latins, the Greeks and the Albanians, just like their languages, stood alone.

It was no accident that Byron loved Albania and Greece equally, just as it was no accident that the Albanians were the neighbors who most significantly helped the Greeks in their struggle for independence. Thousands of Albanian soldiers, officers, generals, and priests fought for Greek freedom as if they were fighting for their own emancipation. There were so many of them that for a time orders were given in Albanian in the Greek ranks, and in one of its first meetings, the Greek parliament engaged in a polemical discussion about whether to institute Albanian as the nation's second language.

Linguistic differences, border disputes, and even Ali Pasha of Tepelena—an Albanian governor who ruled southern Albania and northern Greece, was hated by the Greeks, and was pitied by the Albanians—were unable to sever these Greco–Albanian ties.

The similarities between these two nations and their shared, ancient ancestors became louder during the great agitation that accompanied the liberation from the Turkish yoke. The two nations began to exhume old memories from their national treasure troves, and then it became clear that the new Balkan rage—with its heroic feats, habits, wisdom, assemblies of men, fever, and glory—was colored in striking shades of the past.

The glory lay underneath the foundations of everyday life. It had always been there in Greece, but it was just as present and ran just as deep in Albania, where, as often happens in times of trouble, a part of the treasure had been moved to be safeguarded.

There, in the cold Albanian mountains, epic singers still sang like they had in Homer's time. Older women reminiscent of the Erinyes wore strange garments that resembled those depicted on Mycenaean pots and made sure that young people did not sidestep blood vengeance. In the assemblies of men occurred events similar to those immortalized by Herodotus and Plutarch. Banishments from local provinces, beauty contests for men, the Spartan mentality, and even the "heroic laziness" (*heroische Faulheit*, as the German Gerhard Gesemann calls the passage of time in the mountains)—all these things survived intact in the Albanian mountains.

It seems as though right after the deities abandoned ancient Olympus, Greeks and Albanians began to loot the skies as one would loot a palace. They hastily shredded divine garments, keeping only small bits or tokens. Sometimes they went even further. Albanians tried, for example, to create a new deity in the guise of the "guest," a feeble god whose position anyone could temporarily occupy by getting on the road and knocking on someone's door.

In the Albanian mountains, tragedy could happen over nothing, misery over an insult, and blood vengeance of a hundred years over a careless word.

A scene from everyday life: the family of a recently married woman visits the newlyweds' home, their cattle, and their water-wheel. Even such an ordinary occurrence might contain a fatal surprise for the Albanians. As the proud wife shows the three-story tower, the mill, the guest room, and the guns on the walls, in short, as she displays her hospitality, someone mentions, intangibly, elusively, an old blood loss that has gone unavenged.

The conversation withers despite the wife's attempt to keep it alive. Finally, someone asks what caused the blood loss. The answer—"a woman"—awakens the youth's curiosity but darkens the faces of the elders. They think blood feuds started over women and the murder of dogs have continued for far too long.

The wife realizes that the shadow of death hovers over her three-story stone tower, beautiful paths, and animal pens. The blood feud will follow the men born of her for generation after generation, and there is nothing she can do to stop this fatality.

As though to ease the tragedy of their lives, the Albanians unloaded some of their anger onto their neighbors, the Montenegrins. It was not enough to unburden themselves, though, and they suffered for hundreds of years, like the heroes of antiquity, from open and incurable graves.

Perhaps the name "Accursed Mountains" has its roots in all of this. The mountains could also easily be called the "Mountains of Phaethon." It would be hard to find another place in the world that could have been so readily decorated with a bust of Aeschylus.

There is a striking moment, unparalleled in its grotesquery and courage, in Aristophanes's comedy, *The Frogs*: two groups of dead people engage in a debate regarding the art of the two great tragedians, Aeschylus and Euripides. In order to arbitrate the dispute between the two clans, the judges are obliged to weigh in on the balance of stanzas, imagery, and metaphors between the two rivals. This moment constitutes the first analysis of Aeschylian art. Meaningful in its own right and made not long after the death of the tragedians, this dispute was as prophetic for the victor, Aeschylus, as it was for the loser.

Unwittingly, Aristophanes revealed a fundamental feature of Aeschylus: the tragedian's majestic constructions are made of deep foundations with details of particular value. The weighing of these details—the verses, imagery, and metaphors—allows us to realize that the entire edifice of Aeschylus's literary work, consisting of smaller units, should be considered as treasures.

If we imagine that the core gravitational pull of the mechanism that sets Aeschylus's drama in motion breaks, then the parts of the mechanism that dislodge from the whole still retain their independent value, much like the precious stones of a broken watch. In short, the isolated, raw materials used by the tragedian are resplendent, and when they are integrated into drama their worth only multiplies.

As the offspring of a happy marriage between poetry and drama, Greek tragedy remains beautiful even when its dramatic mechanism does not work perfectly.

In the famous infernal controversy imagined by Aristophanes, Aeschylus is blamed by his adversaries for a cold, frightful, and ominous brilliance. In truth, despite its monumentality, his work is filled with fragile, rainbow-like orchestrations like few others. It is hard to find another playwright with such a wide arc of colors, ranging from the stately black, to the sweeter, brighter tones. The resonance varies surprisingly from place to place within a work, or even within a single scene. Among the black clouds, amid the squabble of deities, macabre feasts, and the axes of crime, one finds the wonderful tranquility of human happiness, the approach of old age, and, of course, the sadness of a man abandoned by his wife.

But alongside these glass verses, in watercolor, one can be suddenly plagued by dark premonitions, murder, and the chorus howling over the cut-up body of the king.

Aeschylus's creation of metaphors is most unexpected and diverse. In order to give Orestes a spiritual blow if he does not avenge his father's blood, the tragedian works with cosmic dimensions, envisioning a time of remorse like a stretch of complete hopelessness. Meanwhile, he creates figures from the tangible, surrounding world—such as livestock, trees, road dust, horse bridles, vessels, and fishermen—with the same ease.

Aeschylus cannot be accommodated by any clichés. Not only the characters, but also their climate and interdependencies are unexpected, gyrating like different stages of a storm. Suffice it to recall here the last part of *Agamemnon*, when Clytemnestra, after spewing venom and hatred against her killed husband, after decrying his murder of their daughter, and after giving orders to bury him without honor, suddenly says:

> I struck him and killed him, I'll bury him too,
> But not with mourners from home in his train,
> No, Iphigeneia, his daughter shall come,
> As is meet, to receive him, her father, beside
> Those waters of wailing, and throwing her arms
> On his neck with a kiss she shall greet him.

The reader is, and rightfully so, surprised at these words. Why would a woman, still trembling from rage against the dead, who, as the chorus says, considers the droplets of blood on her forehead ornamental jewels, declare something so empathetic? Her statement evokes Agamemnon's deep loneliness and the sadness he might feel when the only person to come forward to embrace him is the daughter he sacrificed. Another question arises: why would the girl do this? What would motivate her to greet her killer with open arms?

The questions continue on, and through these inquiries we realize that the tragedian has said something, in passing and mysteriously, that is much larger than our contemptible questions. He has spoken a truth about the reconciliation of the father and his daughter, who both have been wounded at the Trojan campaign, one at the beginning, and the other at the end.

When you step into the world of ancient literature, you realize the naïveté of theses that speak of technological advancement's alleged impact on writing. According to these small minds, the impact of radio, phone, television, aircraft, and space exploration is so significant that it could change the nature of literature. How frivolous is such a thesis! It is enough to read merely the beginning of the second song of the *Iliad* to understand that the great blind one had no need for any TV waves or rocket ships to shift the narrative "camera" from the angry Zeus to the ground, and to the military log about the Trojan campaign. Aeschylus swept over the heads of thousands of soldiers and sleeping commanders to find the sleeping skull of Agamemnon, within which a dream was being conjured.

Let's imagine an extraterrestrial being on whom we impart some knowledge about the Earth and then present two dramas, one ancient and the other modern, without indicating which is which. It is likely that after reading both, when asked to determine which preceded the other, this being might point to the ancient drama as a concoction of modern times and to the contemporary drama as something from antiquity.

The moment when the ancient Greeks suddenly enter the life of a person is akin to experiencing a great earthquake. To some, this happens during childhood. To others, this occurs deep into old age. Like all great convulsions, ancient Greek literature has the unsettling ability to strike us at any stage.

It is known that the ancient Greeks provided a sense of serenity for Voltaire and especially for Schiller and Goethe. If we are to believe his wife's notes, this is not what happened with Leo Tolstoy. She berated him for continually thinking about *his* Greeks, whom she blamed for making her husband ill: "They bring only angst and indifference about today's life. No wonder they call Greek a dead language." Tolstoy himself never claimed that the ancient Greeks brought him turbulence and anxiety, but Countess Tolstoy was convinced that dealing with them was the same as dealing with residents of hell.

We know nothing of what disturbances the Greeks might have occasioned in Shakespeare's soul. We do know that when he wrote his grimmest tragedies, *Macbeth* and *Hamlet*, he was as old as Tolstoy was when the Greeks "sickened" him. We also know that Tolstoy worshipped the Greeks and did not care much for Shakespeare—but let's set these family quarrels aside.

Just like it does within one's life span, the Ancient Greeks inevitably emerge in the life of nations. Seneca was one of the first bridges through which the Greeks of antiquity passed with their blinding lights. They landed in the European continent, and from there moved onward to illuminate the whole world.

This unexpected incursion brought humanity unprecedented new dimensions of thought and imagination. It brought hell, the wounded conscience, Prometheanism, fatality, duplicity, and shadows.

There has been much discussion about the echoes of Greek masters in world literature, beginning with Latin authors, then Dante, Shakespeare, and Goethe, and finally appearing in texts by Hölderlin, Hauptman, O'Neill, T. S. Eliot, and Sartre. There would not be an inferno without the earlier Greek models of hell. What would the bloodstains on the hands of Lady Macbeth look like without the earlier stains on Clytemnestra's hands? What would the disturbed consciences look like, the broken sleep or the unsettling dreams, the glowing candlesticks in the middle of the night? What shape would these crimes have taken?

Despite some progress, much has yet to be explored. It is interesting, for example, to see how Shakespeare's victim-kings, killed by those who aspire to their throne and lust for their women, are not so colorful when compared to the more intricate Agamemnon.

Shakespeare stands the victim-kings alongside their murderers and idealizes the former, which suggests that schematization is such an insidious disease that it can infect even a genius. Aeschylus, quite free from this ailment, gives us the anguish and sorrow of Agamemnon's death while also reminding us of his previous atrocities. In Agamemnon we find both Hamlet and Duncan, the good kings, and Macbeth and Claudius, their killers.

We can still speak of Prometheanism, this tremendous strain on human relationships that does not allow humanity to rest. We can also keep exploring the indirect echoes of Aeschylian literature in writings that at first seem totally unrelated to his works. With the bloody chronicle of the Atreus, Aeschylus began the tradition of reporting the crimes and dramas that defile the homes of big families, a tradition that passed on from drama into prose, eventually making its way into masterpieces by Balzac and Tolstoy. What Aeschylus started in the Atreus, Balzac and Tolstoy continued in upscale Parisian neighborhoods and during the cold Russian winter.

While ancient literature continued to flood the world, its point of origin, the Balkan Mountains, was forgotten.

Aeschylus was reflected in a cold Latin mirror, and violently separated from the Balkan world. Neither Oedipus, Ulysses, nor Orestes were Kabbalistic codes meant to represent eternal human shadows. Before they became archetypes, they were Greeks, ancient Balkan people, born of a certain history and in an environment that set into motion their dramas.

Their dramas began to appear on the stages of Europe, talking and cursing in all kinds of languages at a time when Balkan theaters were silent and taken over by wild grass. The Balkan Mountains were covered by darkness and sadness. Ancient literature's incandescence did not even cast a flickering light on these mountains. The Greeks and the Albanians, the oldest inhabitants of the peninsula, knew nothing about tragedy. But even without knowing tragedy, they wove tremendous sagas plotted by its ancient mechanisms. Theirs was an artistic impulse that rose from the depths of antiquity to capture new elements of life. Its slow fermentation, however, has remained outside the attention of researchers.

When Albert Lord and Milman Parry came to Albania and Southern Yugoslavia in the '30s, the old Homeric workshop was yielding its last products. Pale and somewhat strange, these products were the offspring of old age, but this only makes their investigation more enticing.

Twenty-five centuries after Aeschylus, and nearly five centuries after Shakespeare revived theater, humanity has not yet closed its doors on this particular art form. In fact, the great tragedians are closer to us than ever. There are palaces all over the world awaiting an Aeschylus or a Shakespeare to write of their horrors and intrigues—the Kremlin, the Vatican, the palace of the Borgias, the Chinese Summer Palace, and dozens of temples or other houses whose walls have seen and heard horrors that would make the whole Earth tremble.

We know that Macbeth invited King Duncan for dinner and killed him in his sleep. But the reverse could have easily happened. Duncan, suspecting Macbeth of secret collusions, might have invited the latter to dinner and become the killer rather than the victim.

One night in September of 1971, Mao Zedong invited his Macbeth, Lin Biao, to dine at the Summer Palace . . .

And so the story repeats itself.

*

Nietzsche liked to say that Greek tragedy killed itself. At first sight, a suicidal end fits a genre that only lived about a hundred years—a brief life for an art form.

Over time, as Nietzsche rightly said, tragedy grew aberrant and corrupted. According to him, it was music that first disgraced and silenced tragedy. Next, Olympus withdrew, leaving in its place the creations of Euripides, whom Nietzsche considers the forefather of journalistic thinking. The German philosopher reminds us that Socrates, who was not a lover of tragedy, did enjoy Euripides's more rational plays.

Are we at the moment when things worsen irreversibly? The mysterious but magnificent Aeschylian blur was replaced by the more self-conscious tragedy of Sophocles, and then the latter was supplanted by the primal realism of Euripides. There is something unnatural about this demolition of the order of things. Tragedy itself followed a tragic journey, as though to close a vortex.

The father of comedy, Aristophanes, paid tribute to the darkness the three tragedians conjured by rounding out their trilogies with a fourth, satirical play—much like funeral marches sometimes close with a tune full of zest and hope. To our surprise, Aristophanes praised the imposing beginnings of tragedy and not at all the latter works written by Euripides.

One question remains: did tragedy truly die at such a young age? Perhaps what was taken for death was really a hibernation, a two-thousand-year coma after which tragedy reawakened to find itself in a northern and foggy terrain, the name of which the Greeks did not even know.

William Shakespeare's tragedy moved from the mundane to the perfect, whereas the Greek tragedians' writing moved from perfection to mundanity. Black clouds multiplied year after year in the mind of the Englishman, and cheerful light comedies cleared space for his great darkness.

As he prepares to die, Shakespeare summons death to the stage in one of his sonnets. The playwright walked away from Euripides and toward Aeschylus naturally, as though beckoned by the voice of his origins. He arrived at the source of the tragedy: the funerary rites. The closing scenes of *Hamlet* and *Macbeth* make this very clear.

On March 3, 1585, in Vicenza, Italy, after having seen a performance of *Oedipus Rex*, a critic compared the chorus with the polyphonic music of Balkan funeral cries. Perhaps unconsciously, the music director had felt the need to revisit tragedy's origins, a time when music and crying had held a very important place. But the importance and interconnectedness of music and crying has since lessened in most cultures. Meanwhile, the Balkan people, like the Greeks of antiquity, continued to accompany their funerals with polyphonic wailing. Music, which according to Nietzsche had been embarrassed into silence during the decay of tragedy, lived on through Balkan funeral rites. As if time had stopped, professional criers continued to be a part of funeral rites in the peninsula. The brightness of tragedy, fragmented into tens of thousands of particles, thus hibernated.

There is still no comprehensive research on Balkan funerary lamentations, an essential piece of the history of humanity. There are even fewer investigations on how tragedy ossified within the language of the Balkan people. This happened not only in proverbs and expressions, but sometimes even in the substrate of the language, down to its very foundations. For example, the Albanian causative verb is an unusual grammatical mechanism via which any verb can take on two distinct semantic angles: the virtuous and the evil one. This sense of causality, which was inherited from deep antiquity, gives verbs polar tendencies, so that the Albanian language can be either exalting or terribly destructive.

In the Albanian language, the verb "to be" has the causative form "that I were," which is completely untranslatable. In order to capture its ambiguity, we must break down the form's dualism. "That I were" more or less means "I wish I could be good and just," whereas its other form, "that I were not," means "my being is undesirable, perverse, and unfair." In other words, while in the first case my being is in harmony with the world, in the second case, it disrupts this harmony.

This self-cursing language contains a tragic fatality: it proclaims the transgressive nature of certain states of being. If you are sent, for example, to communicate news to your sister that will bring her great suffering, you might reply, "It is me, but I wish I weren't" in response to her question of, "Who is at the door?" If someone in Colonus had asked the blind Oedipus, "Who are you?" he would reply, "It is me, but I wish I weren't." This response captures the drama of his life, as well as the simultaneous hope that fate had averted many misfortunes by preventing his birth.

Whenever we think about the great tragedies, our mind turns to death—this primary concern of individuals that has resulted in many a desperate campaign. Our fear of death is felt most acutely when we stand around the emptiness of the tomb, where the land meets the sky. This is the rift through which the population of the world passes on to either heaven or hell. As the world's earliest generations moved through this rift, the world grew more prosperous but, due to the absence of these people, more somber. After all, these great, absent people were the luminous protagonists of humankind.

Nietzsche, as though to find solace from the doubts that plagued him, kept returning to these people—the originators of tragedy. And because he could not find any alternative beginnings for tragedy, he repeated the same thesis.

Jean-Pierre Vernant reminds us that according to Plutarch, the public was incredibly shocked that Phrynichus and Aeschylus's tragedies had been included in the Dionysian festival. The justification for their unlikely inclusion has been extensively developed over many centuries. The aimless wandering, escapism, and divine madness of Dionysian feasts and orgies were undoubtedly attractive stages for the poets. When the poets came into conflict with Apollonian restraint, it became more attractive to stage their plays in the uninhibited Dionysian festivals.

The state of intoxication from sex and music that prevailed at these parties was often confused with poetic inspiration, the feasts' unsteadiness and abandon was taken for echoes of a poetic fury directed toward worlds unknown, and the depersonalizing masks worn during the celebrations were compared with the masks of actors, thus permanently forging an umbilical link between these festivals and the tragic theater.

The world of masks has invited much thoughtful and diverse research. Some consider masks a signal of artistic independence and a disdainful separation from reality, but the origin of masks precedes that of art, and masks abound even among people whose theatric gene never developed. In these peoples, masks are a sort of theater that will never emerge from the womb. Others consider masks, especially those with mouths stretched in fear and suffering, to be the places where mortality and immortality meet.

Homer's Odysseus is terrified as he descends into hell and beholds the head of the Gorgon, a visage often depicted in Greek masks. To befall that stony gaze, says Homer, was as bad as becoming one of the dead.

However, if we extract the masks from the Dionysian festival and place them in a funeral rite instead, it is clear that this is where their heavy shadows truly belong. The Dionysian mystery joins the Apollonian quiet in funerary rites, which perhaps means that these rites were the masks' point of origin.

Regarding the mask, it may be difficult to find a true origin for it other than death—and more specifically the face of the dead. Its frozen quality demarcates two kingdoms. Its duality draws us into a mysterious dimension: the deceased is still here, and yet not quite in this world. This duality inspires terror, and even relatives, who only a few hours ago took care of this person lovingly, now fear the cold corpse. If we investigate the open mouth, its distressing emptiness, the mask's focal point, our mind cannot but think of the face of the dead.

The actor who is about to come forward to testify on behalf of the missing person wears a mask on his face. His head is covered by night, according to Homer. He gets closer to the intangible element of the world, making his testimony more disturbing and therefore more believable.

Dionysian parties took place at the end of winter, an appropriate time for open-air theater. There were other reasons that made this schedule obligatory. Spring and summer were full of work, travel, and warfare. So the end of winter was a brief period during which the angst and losses of the passing year were played out on stage and thus remembered.

The theater on the side of the acropolis would slowly fill up with viewers. There were days when the entire city participated in the theater: thousands of words were whispered regarding the choice of plays and jury. The new tragedian to hit the theater scene was either the future of drama or had come to pollute the art form irreparably.

The public discussed the expenses of the production, the effect of the new theater masks, the actor who lost his voice to a cold right before the show, ticket hustling, and many other such issues. This sea of gossip entered the theater's doors along with the people and spread all around.

The theaters of the time were much bigger than the ones we have now. They held over 10,000 viewers. Some even held 15,000 or 17,000 audience members, according to the chronicles.

Everything was rowdy but the audience was also expectant. In the wooden stairs sat high officials, the wealthy, well-known hetaerae, and ambassadors.

Sometimes even prisoners, accompanied by guards, would attend the theater, which proves just how essential theatergoing was considered in ancient Greece. We do not know whether the prisoners had to pay, and if they did whether their currency was silver or if it was their flesh, for a trip to the theater.

Those who had family in prison awaited this opportunity to see them. They would gesticulate to the prisoners and either try to communicate, or simply smile and tear up. Meanwhile, other theater-goers would converse about the winner, fight prematurely, get angry, get offended, or eat the olives they had brought with them.

"Our Aeschylus will win again, just wait and see."

"But there is now also another name on the scene—Sophocles or Euripides, to be honest we are not sure—but they say that these new ones might threaten the old master."

"Nonsense, no one can surpass Aeschylus. Did you say Sophocles? He who in last year's competition played the role of Nausicaa because his voice is so high-pitched? Some dramaturge."

Others talked about all sorts of things. Someone might bring up the collective sum that was to be spent on the Dionysian holidays, for example, and the conversation would then turn to the monetary reward that the winning tragedian would receive. The prize would strike some as substantial and others as less so. It could either support a family for fifteen years, purchase thirty slaves, or be squandered carelessly in a week. Others, getting caught up in this discussion, would remember various curiosities, such as the yearly budget for the Athenian police (forty talents) or the military expenses of a smaller campaign (nearly a thousand talents).

In the meantime, the theater kept filling up and it was now difficult to find a spot. The ambassadors, the archons, the prisoners, in fact even the hetaerae, who usually came last, had all arrived and found a spot on the wooden stairs. Across the stage one could glimpse the actors in passing. Somewhere among the ranks reserved for the famous guests sat the tragedians, who, for one reason or another, could not act in their own plays.

Aeschylus was in this theater for the last time when he was nearly seventy. He was competing with a drama. He was tired of the long war, of all the regrets. He had founded an art form, a second conscience for humanity, but felt like a man leaving his children behind in a cold and dark world. He questioned whether tragedy was valuable, and wondered if it would bring more disturbance than it would benefits.

He saw many things with the eyes of a shadow. The loud noise that echoed in his ears as he sat in the theater informed him that it could and would all continue even in his absence. He did not recognize some of the competitors. One of them, the one about whom the crowd spoke the most, was very young, with beautiful and flowing hair. Aeschylus could not make out the young man's eyes. He was dizzy. At his age, four days of competition were quite tiring.

And now they are nearing the end of the last performance. The break before the vote, the quiet before the verdict, the nearly inhuman voice of the jury declares the victor . . .

It is not his name.

His eyes darken. He would have liked for his ears to fail as well. Outrage had already been brewing in his brain. He had nothing left to say but "To hell with everything." To hell with the theater and dramaturgy. He would not write anymore. In fact, he should have stopped a long time ago. The Greeks did not deserve everything he had done for them. He would burn his manuscripts and everything else at home, any projects, sketches for the future, everything, everything. To hell with everything, but especially with Greece and the Greeks. Cruel, ungenerous country, ungrateful and short-sighted. He had tried to immortalize them all, but they were not worthy of this honor.

He had tried to show another face of them, a nobler face, for their real faces were covered with masks for good reason. He had hoped that in the course of the years he would change Greece gradually, that she would begin to adapt to the mask he had forged.

But Greece spurned his attempts. She preferred her unadorned face, her memories, and her broken laws and consciences.

To hell with everything. He had only one wish: to get as far away from Greece as possible. To never see Greece anymore, to never hear her tiresome complaints. He was going to relocate to the coast of Illyria or even farther still, to the island of Sicily. And he didn't want to hear theater, Athens, or Greece mentioned.

This is how he vented to himself, but even as he tried to cast Greece aside, her weight was on his shoulders. And no matter how much he might foam at the mouth, he could never get rid of her. They would carry one another for millennia. He felt that this bond was fatal, but there was, in all that fatality and darkness, the possibility of light, happiness, and resurrection . . .

(TIRANA, JANUARY 1985; PARIS 2000)

DANTE, THE INEVITABLE

OUR PLANET is much too small to avoid Dante Alighieri. One cannot escape Dante any more than one can escape one's conscience. No other literary work has held humanity, or rather its collapse, in the same way.

In Europe, in that great neighborhood that birthed Dante, everyone has heard the author's name. But the echo of his name stretches to the farthest corners of the world—as far as the United States, Russia, Israel, Japan, Australia, and New Zealand. And if there are places where Dante is not known, then this ignorance is surely a temporary one.

In *The Sacred Wood*, T. S. Eliot writes that Dante's cantos "should be read as a broadening of the strictly limited human space."

The finite nature of our world plagues humanity's great creators. They all try to overcome the limits of our planet, and in their airborne state, some fly farther than others. Dante Alighieri has flown the farthest.

The absence of a land to call his own made him create a kingdom from which he could never be exiled.

It is likely that Florence was at the core of his *Inferno*. His masterpiece could perhaps be traced back to a dream he had while he lived in exile, or even before, when he sensed that he was about to be banished. It was one of those dreams where you are unable to walk, where you try to find something but you cannot reach it, where the terrain is foggy, and where the air and the wind, although they move, are dead.

According to the testimony of Anna Akhmatova, the Russian poet Osip Mandelstam, a fellow citizen of Soviet hell, was most enchanted by Dante precisely on the eve of his own exile. Mandelstam had already begun to feel as though he was living in a Dantesque inferno. To him, hell was a self-contained space. Accordingly, the circles of hell are all the cities where the banished cannot enter. Mandelstam believes that in Dante's writing, Italian cities, like Pisa, Florence, Lucca, or Verona, are "nothing but the Saturn rings of exile," monstrous and nebulous circles that loop around in the storm.

Dante immersed his world within the kingdom he was creating, which expanded day after day and night after night.

One of the first things we learn about Dante is that he was banished from his city. This is the superficial, visible part of his story. But finding ourselves in front of the kingdom with which he replaced Florence, his hell, purgatory, and paradise, we must ask the paradoxical question: is it possible that he sought to intentionally lose his Florence?

A similar question should be asked about his Florentine wife, Beatrice Portinari, who was rather miserly with the poet and died at age twenty-four without, as they say, "becoming his."

For many Dante experts, the lost city and the inaccessible woman are both immured in the foundations of the highest cathedral of poetry, *The Divine Comedy*. Florence is bound up in space, while Beatrice represents time. To Borges, life and time assumed a dual form in Dante's eyes: they either existed with or without Beatrice. He lost her in Florence, and according to his disciples spent the rest of his time trying to create paradise, a place where he could see her again. We must ask, again: is it possible, as with Florence, that Dante viewed the loss of Beatrice as a type of great exchange?

As in no other text, time and space are infinite in *The Divine Comedy*. But Dante wanted to go further still. Dantesque geographical locations, according to some, "are not spaces, but rather psychic states." The three parts of his poem—*Inferno*, *Purgatory*, and *Paradise*—are the three human states that we all experience constantly.

"Born for everyone and brought up by everyone," said Saint-John Perse of Dante on the latter's seven hundredth anniversary.

The cities of Northern Italy revolve in circles around Dante, like the terrifying rings of Saturn about which Mandelstam writes. Italy, too, revolves around him. As do her neighbors, the European continent, and the whole world. One after the other, the circles envelop Rome, Berlin, Lushnja, Magadan, Moscow, Burrel, Budapest, Auschwitz, Tirana, Prague, Babi Yar, and Kolyma.

Willingly or unwillingly, all these places, people, and languages, have established a rapport with Dante that is marked in the skies as permanently as the North Star. Everyone shares a history with him.

In this essay, we attempt to provide a brief history of the relationship between Dante and Albania, one of Italy's closest neighbors.

Separated from Albania by a narrow and shared sea, the Italy we know would grow as inevitable in the Albanian imagination as it was for Dante's soul.

As the exiled Dante Alighieri wrote his *Divine Comedy*, the first Ottoman scouts, looking for a way to attack Europe, appeared in the Balkan peninsula.

As Dante's posthumous fame grew, the Ottomans solidified their power over the Balkan peoples, and the renowned Byzantium, despite its pretense at imperial status, lost everything and became a concubine for the massive Ottoman state.

Years later, when Boccaccio named his *Divine Comedy* after Dante, the Albanian count George Kastriot (also known as Skanderbeg) made a last-ditch attempt to stop the Ottoman wave from washing over Albania. George Kastriot frequently crossed the Adriatic Sea to coordinate his military campaign with his western allies—the Duke of Venice, the King of Naples, and the Roman Pope. At times he traveled alone, and at other times he traveled with an entire military division. These divisions consisted of Albanians fighting intra-Italian wars, or Italian officers helping the Albanians battle against the Ottomans. As might be expected, not all officers made it back home. According to the chronicles of the time, in one of the most tragic of these battles, the Siege of Berat in Albania, the number of Italian soldiers and officers killed neared five thousand.

George Kastriot commanded these joint European troops against a common enemy, making him one of the generals whose nascent efforts constitute the prehistory of all future Atlantic alliances.

Yet neither the many titles Skanderbeg accrued ("protector of Europe" or "athlete of Christendom"), nor the eulogizing biographies, poems, novels, dramas, and operas written about him by famous authors were able to stop the Ottoman advance. The entire Balkan way of life, with its languages, ancient memories, churches, and rites would come to an end. In one of the last battles, during the final siege of the city of Shkodra, the Turkish soldiers used the words "Rome! Rome!" as a war cry. The empire was getting ready to take over Europe, and Mehmet the Second's threat that he would soon tie his horse to the door of St. Peter's Cathedral terrified the entire continent.

The Balkans ceased being part of the European continent. In one stroke, the Albanians lost freedom, Europe, and Dante.

As a Christian and a poet, Dante's existence was doubly impossible in the new empire.

The Ottomans were, reputedly, tolerant tyrants. But what was taken for tolerance was merely a modus operandi driven by the logic of a multinational empire. Willingly or unwillingly, in a giant state made up of many people, races, languages, and faiths, difference had to be tolerated to some extent. But when only some differences are sanctioned, the more dangerous divergences are suppressed. Written language was the Balkan people's most dangerous patrimony, and it was repressed in the most vicious manner. Thousands of teachers and students caught learning and teaching their own language in secret basements were massacred. If other Europeans were aware of this exceptional martyrdom, they might be less surprised at the Balkan cult of language. Dante Alighieri's Christianity would have been sanctioned by the Ottomans, but his dangerous words would have been harshly stifled.

In the Muslim world, Dante only has a small, largely negative space. Dante and Virgil meet the prophet Muhammad in the eighth circle of the *Inferno*, and when Muhammad inquires after Dante's identity in canto 28, Virgil responds: "Death does not have him yet, [. . .] I who am dead must lead him through this Hell from round to round, down to the very bottom."

Dante does not elaborate on Muhammad's sins, but placing him in the eighth circle is an incomprehensible act. Even he whose prophetic vision could penetrate far and wide could not have foretold that this, the smallest of tercets, was going to anger millions of future Muslims.

Virgil and Muhammad give us the impression of two old acquaintances that treat Dante like a novice. Muhammad's question, Virgil's response, and Dante's silence and modest stance in the presence of these two seasoned inhabitants of hell all underscore the strange atmosphere of the poem.

Virgil is as indifferent toward Christianity as he is toward Islam. At the very beginning of the *Inferno*, he sees the old poets, Homer included, and says nothing. Muhammad naturally does not understand why he finds himself in this dark circle of hell, so his question to Dante might also be taken to mean "Who are you, and why did you put me here?" In other words, "Who are you who imagined me here, in such hot waters? Are you in your right mind, young man?" Virgil's response that he is giving the young man his "full experience" is a subtle acknowledgment of the offended prophet's surprise.

A quiet stiffness replaces the brewing black storm that characterizes the rest of the poem—a shift that can be taken as criticism of the period's prejudiced, dominant doctrines. Or perhaps, since we live at a time when harmony among faiths is demanded at all costs, this is simply our preferred interpretation.

Either way, the poetic path is the most secure one for any poet, and Dante is no exception to this rule. In this same eighth circle, Dante gets confused with Ulysses, who, if he had allowed his fieriness to take over, might have complained at the punishment he had received for having orchestrated the Wooden Horse in Troy.

It is unlikely that Ottoman officials ever read Dante. It is also unlikely that any Albanians were able to read Dante, since state repression resulted in an absence of translators capable of transmitting Dante into the languages of the Balkans.

When this barrier fell along with the fall of the empire, the combined history of Dante and the people of the Balkans unfolded.

Last to be separated from the empire, Albania has a chaotic, dramatic, and at times grotesque story. Her longing for Europe, from which she was separated for five centuries, naturally led to the institution of a German prince, William of Wied, as her first king in the time of freedom. World War I found Albania under this prince's rule, but the storms of the war would not only erase this transitional kingdom, they would also turn the country into a true theater. European armies, absent for years and now, as though making up for lost time, emerged forcefully. There were Frenchmen, Austrians, Greeks, Italians, Serbs, groups of Turkish sympathizers, and, naturally, an Albanian army commanded by Dutchmen. By the end of the storm, Albania had become half her original size.

Albanians made peace with their immense loss and declared their independence. Then came the reign of an Albanian king, Zog I. But on April 7, 1939, perhaps to remind Albanians of an old sin, the Italians invaded Albania and removed the king. That same month, an Italian king was crowned. Victor Emmanuel III assumed the official title of emperor of Ethiopia and king of Italy and Albania. It seemed as though Albania had finally been singled out for greatness, but of a distorted, nightmarish kind. While the boundaries of the new kingdom were spreading all the way to Africa, Albania shriveled and grew smaller.

The Albanians found themselves sharing a state with the Ethiopians, which they interpreted as a racial insult given how much time they had spent hysterically glorifying their own heritage as the noblest in the Balkans. The second surprise was more pleasant, however. Under the shared crown, Italy provided, as dowry: Dante Alighieri. Since a union between states was a solemn matter, before offering music, paintings, or any of its other treasures, Italy shared with the Albanians her spiritual master, the founder of her language, and the symbol of her unity—the poet-prince, Dante. Dante Alighieri, the divine, prophetic, unifying, and official poet of Italy, became the first poet of the Albanians.

Now that Dante was hers, Albania prided herself in him more than anybody else, and even placed his portrait alongside her icons.

Italian propaganda could find no miraculous mechanism that would better attract the Albanians. There were tens of translations, publications, reading groups, initiatives, charity foundations, competitions, forums, streets, and plazas that bore the name of

Dante Alighieri. Albania was decorated everywhere with Dante. The Germans never thought of doing this with Goethe and Beethoven. The circumstances were different, but they also had less faith in these artists then they did in their Panzer tanks and Luftwaffe planes.

Italy unloaded Dante's portraits (along with military flags, kitchen tools, and field cannons), and placed the prince of poetry in the midst of a small country's storm. He, the prince of conscience and the punisher of sinners, conquering Caesars, violators, and liars, had to help the Italians suffocate another people. He was called upon not just to suffocate the Albanians, but to asphyxiate while seeming to caress, while whispering in the ear: "Albania is in my heart, we are a family, we share poetry . . . "

It was a state, to use Dante's own words, that closely resembled the inferno he himself had created.

Time would show that the Albanians, normally stern and prone to holding grudges, had no conflicts with the poet. The Albanians had loved Dante for a long time, and being occupied by the Italian state could not interfere with this love.

According to Ernest Koliqi, a Dante expert and Albanian anti-communist writer who fled Albania after the Italian occupation, the first translations of Dante were published in the nineteenth century by the Italo-Albanian Luigi Lorecchio. In 1900, Sokol Baçi, an erudite Albanian from Shkodra, translated the fifth canto of the *Inferno*. One of the first translations was of the eleventh canto of *Paradise*. Father Vinçens Prenushi, a poet and dignitary, who tragically died in a communist prison, translated this canto shortly after Albanian independence. During the 1930s, there was an explosion of Dante through translations, many of which were penned by Koliqi himself.

Known for their tendency to move haphazardly between tasks, Albanians, despite their passion for Dante, struggled to fully translate *The Divine Comedy*. Perhaps the children of the eagles were hindered because this magnificent poem aligned so closely with their troubled natures. For instance, within the *Inferno*, which many of them were obsessed with, they would jump from one circle to the other depending on which circle reflected their psychological state, grudges, or hostilities of the moment.

Unlike Shakespeare and Cervantes, whose *Hamlet* and *Don Quixote* became accessible in their entirety at the same time in Albania, Europe's other genius was entering Albanian life through pieces, droplets, variants, and endless citations and comments. We cannot say that this was ideal, but we also cannot say decisively that it wasn't. Dante would become popular in a way that resembled the dissemination of oral poetry. At the time, Dante's *Inferno* resembled the black chronicles of Albanian newspapers. Few translators felt compelled to near *Purgatory*, and fewer still attempted to translate *Paradise*.

There has been much discussion about the Albanians' unique, shared sensibilities with Hamlet, who reminded them of their blood code, or with Don Quixote, in whose portrait they saw, as if through a mirror, their own previous deliriums. The Albanian disorder also fit well within Dante's world.

In Rome, in the sad calm of exile, Ernest Koliqi explored these ties. The notes he left behind, a survey of Albanian and Italian literary studies he carried out at the University of Rome, where he taught, are doubly precious. They are sophisticated and free of the clichés that plague Dantean studies, and they are informed by the author's exile, which acts as a nearly umbilical tie and is akin to the connection that exists between translators and their masters.

Ernest Koliqi writes about the Dantesque manner of thinking and the passionate nature of the Italian master's poetry. In the meantime, the current climate in Albania reflects the turmoil of

Dante's Florence: from the mix of passions and unbridled ambitions, to the factions, explosions of violence, infighting between tribes, prosecutions, and cruel exiles.

Koliqi writes that the traces left in the Albanian memory by three empires—Roman, Byzantine, and Ottoman—made it easy for Albanian students to grasp the historical and political implications of Dante's poem. The conflicts between the sultan and the defiant Albanian feudal lords were similar to clashes that occurred during Dante's Italy. According to Koliqi, while the students understood these fights well, they had a harder time grasping the infighting between the emperor and the pope, since the chronicles of the Ottoman Empire provided no useful analogies for wars between the faith and the state.

Koliqi touches on other poetic similarities between Dante's universe and the unsettled Albanian psyche. The scholar was quite familiar with the old Albanian ballads, where the similarities are obvious even from afar. In them, characters travel through the netherworld and return from the dead. The dead return for three days or a week in order to finish something left undone, usually an unfulfilled promise. There are also wills and promises, premonitions and news sent from the land of the dead to that of the living with the help of birds, clouds, or cuckoos. Just like *The Divine Comedy*, the Balkan ballads are full of outcries: "Oh you crows eating my flesh!" "Oh you wind, oh you clouds." "Do this or that." "Send my well-wishes to my mother." "Return my ring to my bride." "When you go to the field of Rmaj, look for my grave." "If my mother asks for me, tell her this or that."

The inhabitants of Dante's hell are full of similar memories and pangs. Their mind stays with their earthly lives, they want to know what happens up there. Neither their frustrations nor their traumas leave them.

The dead, with their grievances and burdens, resemble people in exile. Dante sketched out the magnificent and sad landscape of migration that Europe, and later the whole world, would experience. The Balkan people, in particular the Greeks and the Albanians, who according to their old customs would craft touching ballads about this "new migration," saw exile as a half-death, since half of those who left would never return.

In no other narrative is the true nature of exile, with its landmarks of hell and purgatory, captured as it is by Dante. The inhabitants of his hell closely resemble migrants. The fragments of stories, the burdens, the anger, the political curiosity, the thirst for news, the wills and testaments, and the regrets all seem to emerge from the same psychic makeup. In fact, if we somehow switched Dante's poem with today's narratives, readers might have trouble distinguishing *The Divine Comedy* from the chronicles of our time.

What is going on in Rome, is there peace or war? We took off from Durrachio, but drowned in Otranto. Remember me; I am from Pia. I was made in Sienna and undone in Marena. Light a candle for me in the field of Rmaj. No one responded to any of my letters while the internment truck came along. What happened in Tirana, who won the elections? Guelphs or Ghibellines?

The droning of the city—the street names, addresses, requests, wastelands where souls have left the body, curses, polemics, caves where the subways of the future breathe alongside graffiti— tempted Dante since he himself, anytime he runs across someone from Florence, cannot help but ask whether they might know a young woman by the name of Beatrice Portinari.

The scene is astounding. The poet, proud of his vow never to mention the dead Beatrice until he is able to write of her as no woman has been written about, feels the need to speak about her even if it is only with a wanderer of the inferno. And this is not all.

Cruel with himself, he records the indifferent denial of the other in order to show that she who was the center of his life is nobody to the wanderer.

After 1,700 years, Dante returns the majestic commotion of Greek tragedy to world literature. But while in the ancient theater the chorus was responsible for the texts' polyphony, in Dante's poetry it emerged from the groaning of the endless number of the dead.

He was the first who managed to capture the future noises of the cities of the world. They would bring about a civilization that began precisely in the depths of Dante's vision of hell, or, in other words, with the struggles of conscience.

There is no good answer to the question of whether the Italian vernacular was too "vulgar" to carry the weight of the Dantesque world, or whether it was Dante's own path that was linguistically self-limiting. The phenomenon is unique in the history of humanity: on the eve of its birth, a new language gave rise to a poem characterized as "divine," the likes of which has not been produced since.

Before developing histories with every country in the world, Dante established his first, most incredible tie with his own people, the Italians. Dante's history with Italy can be summed up in a few lines: A people and a man work together to create something special—a cathedral, an intoxicating sky. The two of them, the people and the man, like the Virgin Mary and the Holy Spirit, then give birth to a miracle.

Dante's other acquaintances, with whom he had stormy histories of understandings and misunderstandings, would come subsequently.

Ernest Koliqi's last observations are notes about the rendition of Dante in Albanian. He describes the trajectory of the poet's connection to the Albanians—first the Albanians' forty-year adoration, then their forty-year condemnation, and finally Dante's rebirth in contemporary Albania. Gjergj Fishta, according to Koliqi's writings, considered Albanian "our masculine language," an especially appropriate medium to convey Dante's proud expressions.

Unfortunately, neither Fishta nor Koliqi explained this idea any further.

In his notes about Dante, Ernest Koliqi never mentions any other similarities, not even the resemblances between the Nazi concentration camps, the communist gulag, and the Dantesque world. When those places were first discovered, mouths numb with horror must have uttered the word "Dantesque."

Koliqi's notes date to the 1970s, a time when these terrors had already been uncovered. At a first glance, the absence of any reference to them seems surprising. Even more surprising is his failure to mention, even if in passing, his own burden as a political exile— a burden that connects him, the translator and admirer, with the object of his admiration.

But what initially seems surprising makes more sense from up close. Ernest Koliqi had a connection with Italian fascism. In the 1930s and 1940s, he was renowned for his fascist ideologies. There is nothing fascist in his literary work, not even the slightest sympathy for the Italy of his day, but this was different in real life. After the unification of Albania and Italy, he accepted a position in the Ministry of Culture, in the puppet Albanian government.

He never provided an explanation for this tragic choice. It seems as though a grave misunderstanding about Albania's European future sent him to Rome. Unlike other Albanian writers, many of them his friends, who sang hymns to an isolated and pure Albania, he admired the Italian alliance. Reviving Albania's historic ties with Venice, Rome, and the Vatican, which had been severed by the

Ottoman invasion, seemed to him, as a Catholic, the only way for Albania to return to Christian Europe.

It is not difficult to imagine what the communists would have done to Ernest Koliqi had they caught him. Another poet who shared his sin, the American Ezra Pound, was caught and labeled a traitor.

Naturally, being caught by the Albanian communists was an entirely different thing than being caught by the Americans. Even so, the latter behaved rather cruelly with Pound. Neither his fame, friendships, nor well-known naïveté helped him. Subjected to the mockery of passersby and locked in a cage under a bright light like a wild animal, he who many scholars consider the best twentieth-century poet of the English language lived through something worse than any nightmare.

After the storm, Ezra Pound and Ernest Koliqi—both exiled, one famous in a large country and the other famous in a small country—ended up in post-fascist Italy. Koliqi lived in Rome, while Pound lived in Rapallo, in the north.

It was as unlikely that Pound knew of Koliqi as it was likely that the Albanian admired the great poet. Both were lonely, but what truly brought them together was their connection to Dante Alighieri.

Both had dealt with Dante their whole lives, and in their exile more so than ever. Not only did they feel a sense of kinship with Dante, but the poet was like a church of sorts for them, a place for confession and spiritual purification.

Koliqi remained connected to the great master throughout his youth, boyhood, and later miseries. For much of his life, Ezra Pound tried to erect a tower parallel to *The Divine Comedy*. Trapped in a horrible cage, the idea of hell never left Pound. That cage, which resembled a fortress of conscience, seemed to have been built by Dante.

Both dealt with their idol until the end of their lives, but neither ever spoke about their own hell. In fact, in his essays about Dante, Ezra Pound not only endeavors to escape the *Inferno*, but also tries to convince himself and others that the third part of the poem, *Paradise*, is the most beautiful one.

It is difficult to believe that paradise awaited the two poets after their journey through purgatory. Perhaps they only ever dreamed of paradise.

From Verona, Dante Alighieri petitioned Florence several times to allow his return. His pleas were never heard. Several famous poets wrote appeals on behalf of Ezra Pound, as well, but these also went unheard.

Fate was even crueler with Ernest Koliqi. It was inconceivable that Albania would respond to a petition of mercy issued on his behalf. Albania had cursed herself. Mercy was impossible.

Surprisingly, the muck thrown at Koliqi's name did not stick. It seemed that the Albanians were used to these attempts to defame authors, and even well-known writers of the communist world were often considered "decadent, reactionary, anti-socialist, anti-populist, or anti-party" simply on account of an "ideological error." State-sanctioned defamation paradoxically cast a shadow of secret respect on the writer.

There was, however, another reason why Koliqi avoided being termed a traitor: while he served as Minister of Culture in the fascist government, he managed to open Albanian schools in Kosovo. Albanian schools in places that forbade the Albanian language were more precious than any religious temple, and to open these schools was considered a sacred mission.

Koliqi seemed like a character who had emerged from *Purgatory*. To the Albanian consciousness, he was purified and existed somewhere between being cursed and blessed. This was also why public opinion sided with him since the first day after the fall of communism. Ernest Koliqi was eventually rehabilitated.

It was rehabilitation, this dream and this nightmare, that must have followed him in the course of the thirty-year emigration he described in his sorrowful drama, *The Roots Move*. In his drama, he foretold that the 1970s would witness his own death in exile and the fall of communism. Of both prophecies, only the first one took place right away; the second one would take fifty years.

What is surprising in Koliqi's drama is its strange atmosphere. It is Sunday and the bells of the big Catholic church of Shkodra are ringing again after so many years of silence. The previous regime has fallen. The people remember the exiled writer with nostalgia, saddened that he could not know the excitement of freedom. The writer's rehabilitation took place in a restrained and almost cold atmosphere. From all the readings of the drama, the most compelling advances the theory that this was written by an inhabitant of purgatory—where suffering is painless and happiness is mirthless.

When communism fell in Albania, life was more generous toward Ernest Koliqi than he had ever been to himself. His rehabilitation was immediate and not ambivalent. Year after year, season after season, and week after week, Koliqi had followed the events of communist Albania. He had known full well what was happening there. Many of his friends and relatives had been in prison or work camps; some of them had died from a bullet to the neck. He wrote about these extraordinary horrors many times, he participated in the meetings of the Pan-club of Europe, and in the quiet of Rome, he followed the fate of his idol—Dante Alighieri.

He remembered well those unforgivable days right after the capitulation of Italy. Everything was falling and burning into nothing as he tried to leave. The broken letters of the old empire were being taken away, and countless emblems and signs were being pulled down, including those that bore the name of Dante. Thousands of Italian soldiers—left without anyone to answer to—wandered around the villages and cities of Albania. It was now their turn to ask: Any news from Rome? I am from Florence, but I left my arm in Tepelena. Are the ships coming, or are we going to die here?

Two threats hung on the necks of these soldiers: on the one hand, the famous Albanian sense of vengeance, and on the other, the German troops that came like a dark cloud from the Greek border to execute both their former allies and the deserters. The second fear proved unfounded. Instead, reality took a course that can be interpreted as either a noble or cynical one. The Albanians did not touch their former occupiers, they simply turned the majority of them into servants. It is unclear whether this was an act of hospitality, a crafty humiliation, or a manifestation of their infamous racism. Eventually the Albanians would fall prey to racial hatred themselves, but their short memories did not realize that they were paying for old sins.

From the land of exile where he had settled, Ernst Koliqi followed the Albanian chronicle. He was convinced that the suppression of the Italian language would free the way for Russia, at which point the political storm would surely drag him away. To his great surprise, this did not happen immediately. Even later, when after the Germans' departure the communists managed to finally establish a dictatorship, this did not happen.

Only Dante was left standing. In the midst of Albanian communism, the most vicious regime, the most faithless and alien to Dante, the poet's work was being translated more fully and more masterfully than ever.

At first glance, this seems paradoxical. But then one realizes that Dante Alighieri was being translated more fully and more lovingly precisely because his translators, like the rest of Albania, were experiencing one of his three states, that of hell.

He was born for everyone, but there was a wide area of the world, the sad communist empire, whose people, hopeless and brought to their knees, needed him the most. He was needed by the Albanians, Hungarians, Russians, Jews, Slovaks, Czechs, Poles, the people of the Baltics, Ukrainians, Romanians, Georgians, Armenians, and South Slavs.

In the solitude of exile, Ernest Koliqi learned the big news. He even learned the translator's name, Pashko Gjeçi, who, like Koliqi, came from Shkodra and was a Catholic. He had been in the communist prisons, done forced labor in the stone quarries, and then finally been freed. No one knew which of the "three states" he experienced as he penned his majestic Albanian translation of *The Divine Comedy*.

All this, in particular the publication of the translation, seemed as incredible as a dream and as vulnerable as a mirage to Koliqi. A miracle had taken place in the land of sin where the cross had been dropped to the ground and where there was neither mercy nor sympathy for anyone.

The Divine Comedy was quite foreign to this communist wasteland. And yet, it was also the only gospel and, however wounded, the only conscience left.

Like any dream, the miracle of Dante Alighieri in Albania is coupled with the fear that it might evaporate. It may have been precisely due to this fear that Koliqi never mentions the dangerous similarity between the poem and Albania. A remembrance, someone's denunciation, or a ruse from the dictator, and Albania would lose Dante for a half a century. And worst of all, he would be lost precisely when Albania needed him the most.

There is a "Dante hour" just as there is an afternoon, dawn, or evening. This is the moment when people, governments, epochs, kingdoms, republics, races, and different languages encounter

Dante after having been moving toward him for years. The storms of our planet might push against this hour, but they can never stop it from coming.

At the beginning of the 1940s, after Dante Alighieri gained a second homeland under dramatic and grotesque circumstances, the poet found himself, thanks to this new homeland, bordering Greece, a country that knew him rather well.

Although Greece had been first to be liberated from the Ottoman Empire, Dante's meeting with her, just as with the other Balkan people, was delayed. In 1966, the poet Giorgos Seferis complained that there was still no Greek translation of *The Divine Comedy*.

In 1939, during the unification between Albania and Italy, the old Greco–Albanian border turned into a Greco–Italian–Albanian border. Greece found herself adjacent to the fascist empire, which not only showed off the old Roman insignia, but also aggressively announced its rebirth. And the rebirth of Rome meant a reoccupation of the Balkans and, naturally, of Greece as well.

In the meantime, the two capitals, Rome and Tirana, were inflamed. Little Albania, still recovering from what some had called an invasion and others a unification with Italy, had barely come to terms with the fact that she was in the midst of a new adventure. In seedy bars, just like in masked balls, delirious dialogues seemed endless. It was no accident that the ancient city of Butrint, where the Trojans had made their first stop on their way to Italy, was located in Albania. Mussolini himself followed the archaeological research conducted in Butrint, even though the name of the Italian archaeologist, Ugolini, was reminiscent of an annoying occupant of Dante's hell.

Now the time had come for the Trojan revenge! (Four hundred years ago, sometime after the occupation of Constantinople, the Turkish sultan, Mehmet II, in his first speech, declared that the grandsons of the Trojans, *supposedly* the Turks, were finally avenging their forefathers against the Greeks.)

Troy found grandchildren everywhere, and the Albanians, known as they were for blood vengeance, did not let the opportunity to join their fate to that of an ancient people slip by.

Military preparations were underway. A great fog hung over the war. What kind of war would this be? Between Italy and Greece? Between the united Italian and Albanian kingdoms? Or simply between the two old Balkan goats—the Greeks and Albanians? In the smoky cafés of these neighboring countries, the people speculated that the latter scenario was the most probable one.

In Tirana, old passions were reemerging. After the unification with Italy, Albania had regained Kosovo. It seemed natural that after the war with Greece it would also regain the other region, her Southern loss, Çamëria. Albania was becoming broader, some said. Others insisted on the opposite, and felt that Albania was melting away.

In the meantime, the press was inundated with nostalgic memoirs about Ali Pasha of Tepelena, the Albanian tyrant who ruled over Northern Greece for more than forty years. Anti-Greek racism was rampant. True and false stories of betrayals were being dug out of the archives—the Greek parliament's rejection of Albanian as Greece's second language, for example.

The music of war was growing deafening on the other side of the Adriatic. In his cabinet in Italy, Benito Mussolini leafed through the concocted scenarios in order to find a pretext for war. In his minister's office in Tirana, Ernest Koliqi was giving a last look at a literature textbook that was to be taught at the first Albanian schools in Çamëria. Benito Mussolini's finger hovered over the word "murder." To the Balkan people, nothing is as incendiary as murder. In the margins, Mussolini adds "the murder and betrayal of an Albanian."

Not even forty-eight hours go by and the radios and newspapers in Tirana and Rome are all swarming with the news. In a village next to the Greek border, an Albanian has been treacherously murdered.

The two capitals of the empire grit their teeth. The threatening name of the Albanian capital, "Tirana," which sounds like "tyrant," must have been formulated for this occasion. Every café is abuzz:

"There will be war without a doubt."

"Just like in Sarajevo in 1914."

"But in Sarajevo it was a crown prince that was murdered, Archduke Ferdinand, if I'm not mistaken, while this man was only a villager."

"You forget that above all else he is an Albanian, and Albanian blood is never forgotten. The whole world knows this."

The avalanche of pride set in motion by the ancient code that dictates that this spilled blood not be forgotten for more than four hundred generations easily captures the imagination. Old stories revolve in memory. People remember and newspapers proudly publish the Albanian archbishop's reputed response to a Chinese ambassador's remarks. The latter, surprised that so small a country could create such a racket at the League of Nations, supposedly said: "The entire population of Albania is as small as the number of people that drown in our rivers every year." To which the archbishop replied, "Do not forget, your excellency, that these are Albanian and not Chinese people."

Racial hatred directed at the Chinese would have become more fashionable if there had not been more immediate concerns. The most urgent business was blood vengeance. An Albanian had been murdered! This sound reverberated as though the end of the world had come, as though this was the first murder in the history of humanity. It was momentarily forgotten that the sons of the eagle are often murdered over the most banal reasons, such as a careless word uttered at a café or even just for bothering someone's dog. More than a thousand mad and incredible reasons could have been at the root of this murder.

But all of this was forgotten. An Albanian had been murdered! Let the world know that when an Albanian is murdered, doomsday occurs.

On October 28, 1940, troops of the Italo–Albanian army crossed the border. In reality, it was mostly a series of Italian regiments with a sole Albanian battalion in their midst, the "Tomor."

A single battalion, but an entirely Albanian one nonetheless.

Dante Alighieri, Europe's greatest poet, called an "eternal model" by some and a Christian Homer by others, arrived at Greece in the unusual company of this army.

Would Greece welcome him triumphantly, as her sneaky neighbor to the north had? Would we see a repetition of the same luxurious publications, clubs, forums, associations, competitions, galas, and hundreds of little girls baptized Beatrice? At the end of the day, did Greece even need another Homer?

It seemed as though the answer was bound to be a negative one. Greece had her own great poets. Beyond that, Greece treated Hellenism, a product of the official Italian education that depicted the Greeks as the butchers of the Trojans, indifferently. They had not forgotten that this signor Alighieri had put all the Greek poets, with Homer at their head, in the first circle of hell.

No, Dante had no chance in Greece, and what little chance he'd had of settling on Greek soil had been obliterated by this war. The Italo–Albanian kingdom could win the war, but her first poet was sure to be defeated. Unlike what had happened in Albania, where after the capitulation of fascism Dante had emerged the only real winner, in Greece he could only be a loser.

We know how the passions of the fall of 1940 played out militarily on the world scene. The inflamed imperial dreams of the time were epilogued by the Albanian–Greek border: a giant swamp where holes, barbed wire, and sunken cannons were interspersed with the corpses of mules and young men.

Two great Greek poets of the time, Giorgos Seferis and Odysseus Elytis, found themselves in the midst of this gyrating whirlpool of a war. The first, a leading diplomat in the Albanian city of Korça, not only experienced in a traumatic fashion the passions of war, but likely even reported on them. The second, an officer of the Greek army, had taken part in the counterattack and later marched into Albanian land—a campaign that begat his masterpiece, *To Axion Esti*. Both poets witnessed the sad tableau of the Albanian–Greek boundary, where it seemed as though the poet of hell, Dante, was stuck in the mud, ditches, and barbed wire.

Seferis, the older of the two Greek poets, speaks of the boundary of language in a beautiful homage to Dante. Language, he says, is a secret barrier more powerful than even barbed wires. Dante was trapped in this invisible boundary of language. Giorgos Seferis writes of the regret he experienced from having only encountered the great Florentine poet late in life due to his not knowing Italian. This regret recalls another story that takes places in the mysterious and enigmatic realm of languages.

At the beginning was Italian . . . Without any doubt, she always sits at the origin. But at the same time, it would not be a mistake to say: in the beginning there were two, Dante and Italian.

It is hard to think of another poet with a similar relationship to language. It would have to be an Oedipal relationship, since Dante was at the same time Italian's child and parent. The relationship is even more convoluted than this. It is a mysterious form of initiation.

At times, Dante's history with Italy seems to belong to his other mystery, that of Beatrice. The association is, no doubt, nebulous and intangible until the very end. At other times, it seems as though Dante managed to do with Italian what he never accomplished with Beatrice Portinari. Just like a young girl who in the midst of love and reproduction becomes a new woman, so Italian, carrying within herself the poet, gave birth to *The Divine Comedy*—a creature unlike any it had birthed in its 750 years of life.

The similarities between language and love become more visible if we recall Latin, the serious lady the poet abandoned for the young, lowbrow girl. The criticism his choice inspired and the occasional indifference of his young lover only push the parallel further.

This is what happened with Italian. Out of Dante's history with tens of other world languages this is, no doubt, the most nebulous and least accounted for. The journey of this divine nightmare into translation is itself dark and incomprehensible. It is virtually impossible to imagine the process via which the poem was translated into a foreign language. It is difficult to understand, too, the disorder that Dante's poem must have caused, the efforts to appropriate and adopt the original text that it doubtlessly inspired, and the transformation that the host language underwent as a result of its dangerous guest.

In thinking about Dante and world languages, we cannot help but wonder which language was used in his three kingdoms. The language of choice would need to facilitate conversations among people from different centuries and countries, people both real and fictitious. Through this language they are able to communicate everything and nothing with each other. From this perspective, what we understand as "translation" in the context of Dante's poem could be seen as a realization, and a reworking of material that only came to exist as a result of the greatest poetic catastrophe. Finally, this chosen language could be seen as a request, a plea from the spirits who seek expression in some language or other.

Dante's disciples insist that he cannot be understood in a language other than Italian. Some, like Giorgos Seferis, even think that one needs to know the particularities of Florentine Italian.

During the 1930s, Seferis was a diplomat in the Albanian city of Korça, one of those provincial cities that light-mindedly aspired to be a "small Paris," the likes of which there were always plenty in the Balkans. Wintertime in Korça surprised the poet with its snow, continental frost, and with a particularity of the seasonal assemblies. In Parisian-styled balls, the poet, for whom glory was still ahead, must have enviously ground his jaws at the ease with which the vain and somewhat light-minded local ladies would cite Dante's verses in perfect Italian. He himself would never dare to do this, even though his understanding of Dante, with whom he felt he shared a fraternal bond, was a thousand times deeper than theirs.

It seems as though this fluency was neither accidental nor a grotesque sideshow of which there was so many in the Balkans. This is one of the dark caves of that mysterious entity that we referred to earlier: the world of languages. This one is a particularly unusual, thoroughly studied, and obstinately murky relationship. We have two languages, Italian and Albanian, that seem to have nothing in common. And yet Albanians, naturally and without any particular preparation, understand Italian fairly well, whereas Italians do not understand the Albanian language at all. An Albanian text in their eyes is as dark as a text in Hungarian or Norwegian.

And this is true for everyone—cooks, academics, mechanics, bankers, nuns, or prostitutes. This has happened throughout the history of political systems in Albania—during the republic, at the beginning and end of the king's reign, during fascism, during communism, and even during times of freedom. This happened before Italian television became so beloved in Albania. In fact, it predates the invention of television altogether. This phenomenon did not change with the rise of Albanians' racist sentiments toward the Italians, or when the roles were reversed and the Italians were prejudiced against the Albanians.

The mystery of this rapport between two languages calls to mind the one-way mirror of a witch—one party can see through it, while the other cannot make out anything.

This linguistic mystery helps us understand why the barbed wire lining the Albanian border could not keep out Dante any more than it could keep out the Greek language, which did not enter as readily as the poet. No matter the relationship between the countries, the Albanian language always reached an understanding with Dante. Fishta and Koliqi's statements that pointed to an affinity between Dante and the Albanian language were proven beyond a doubt.

While reading bilingual texts, thousands of young Albanians in schools naturally transitioned between the Albanian translation and the Italian original. Sometimes they had the impression that they were reading a single language wearing different masks.

> *Quivi perdei la vista e la parola;*
> *nel nome di Maria fini', e quivi*
> *caddi, e rimase la mia carne sola.*

> *Dhe humba mend e gojë, ngadalë tue mekun,*
> *shpirtin e dhashë me emnin e Marisë*
> *ku rashë unë mbeta vetëm mish i vdekun*

> Here sight and speech
> Fail'd me, and finishing with Mary's name
> I fell, and tenantless my flesh remain'd.

CANTO 5, *PURGATORY*

This is a freely translated stanza, whereas there are thousands of lines that sound just like the original:

> *e caddie come un corpo morto cade*
>
> *dhe rashë ashtu si trup i vdekur bie*
>
> like a corpse fell to the ground

CANTO 5, INFERNO

The temptation to translate Dante was so great that even Mark Ndoja, a communist writer, in fact a high director of the Albanian League of Writers, left Soviet poetry by the wayside to occupy himself with Dante. He translated *Inferno* and *Purgatory* and eventually ended up in prison. It was never known whether translating Dante got him imprisoned, or if prison made him gravitate toward Dante.

When the author of this essay was thirteen or fourteen years old, he found himself, just like thousands of other schoolboys, facing an unusual linguistic phenomenon that pleasantly confused his young brain. It was two cantos that could be found anywhere—in literature books, magazines, and even newspapers. This is the canto about Paolo and Francesca, the tragic lovers who could never find peace amidst the storm of the second circle of hell, and the canto of Count Ugolini, the inhabitant of the ninth circle of hell who ate his own children in his desperate hunger. At the time, Albanian children could not have been familiar with the suppositions that were later extrapolated from this song's darkness. Did Count Ugolini eat his own children in the tower of hunger or was the whole scene simply a mirage of the imagination? Borges, who wrote one of the most beautiful essays on Dante, feels that the children's begging their father to "strip them of the flesh in which he clothed them" rings a false note. But Borges, who adored

Dante and like him was rarely mistaken, would not have considered this declaration so unlikely if he had been familiar with the conditions of Albanian children. For children, being eaten alive is a daily fear that they inherit along with other atavisms. To be eaten by their father is less scary than many other means of death they were threatened by.

I bring up this example in order to illustrate that the early readings of Dante's work were not always rosy in nature.

The bilingual nature of the text, its sprint, with one language being figuratively thrown over the shoulder of another, can cause mistakes and incidents that leave their traces in time. But for the most part, these mistakes are beautiful ones. For instance, one particular misunderstanding of the line "seguito 'l terzo spirito al secondo" (the third spirit followed the second) for years embedded in the author of this text the idea that in *The Divine Comedy* there are characters with two or perhaps three spirits. Disappointment always ensued upon reading the Albanian version.

Like every story, the brief history of Albania with Dante Alighieri requires a conclusion. Due to the nature of this history and to its circular evolution, reaching a conclusion is not easy.

If we are to start from the loudest and most visible things, then we must start with the war in the midst of this history.

The Balkan peninsula is well-known for its delirious wars, where imagined conflicts become real and lost battles are taken for victories. Regarding the mess in which Dante was entangled, although there was an Italian–Albanian–Greek war, the conflict between Greece and Italy came to a close with the end of World War II, whereas the fight between the Albanians and Greeks continued on. Although it was to be expected that intra-Balkan feuds would be more stubborn than their enmities with more distant peoples, it is nonetheless surprising that this grotesquery has continued for so long, to the point that even today, in the summer of 2005, while I am writing these lines, nothing has really ended, and Albania and Greece remain in a state of semi-war.

Albania, after the Italian occupation and the tyranny of King Zog, was invaded by the Germans in 1943, who declared their invasion Albania's liberation from Italy. After a series of "liberations," Albania would undergo yet another emancipation in 1991, this time orchestrated by fate.

All eras seek something that they do not have, a sort of excess or soulfulness.

We undoubtedly have to count Dante Alighieri among those that embody what our era lacks, and with whom our hope lies. He is there to cleanse us, fix us, or, more likely, to give us the opportunity to suffer in the mirror he placed before us.

The aspiration of little Albania to have a unique history with Dante Alighieri should not be seen as an attempt at appropriation, even if this was one of the region's well-known tendencies. After all, to have a unique history with Dante means to volunteer oneself to suffer.

In this essay, we explored the centenarian file shared between Dante and Albania: the similarities between poetic motifs and human passions, the nearly sensual tendency of the Albanian language to absorb the poet's tercets, the crown shared by the two kingdoms, and finally the new regime that joined Albania with the communist landscape.

In the endless communist expanse that stretched from Tirana to Murmansk and from Berlin to Kamchatka, one could feel a geographic shortage and a striving for a secondary, infernal map that could be charted from the depths in accordance with Dante's older project. Visionary minds, beginning with Kafka, Mandelstam, and even Solzhenitsyn, could discern this truth. The penal colonies, the Saturnian rings, and the gulag archipelago were some of the landmarks of this new camp. Every communist country brought its own emblems. During the education theory period in China, prisoners often cheered much more passionately for the communist party than anyone on the other side of the prison walls. In the majority of places, the space inside and outside prisons tended to become one and the same, so much so that it was difficult to discern in which of the two spaces hope had been most extinguished. In Soviet Russia, the living and the dead shared the same grave. In Czechoslovakia, despite its relative liberalism, for a few years the expression "good morning" was forbidden; it was officially replaced with "glory to labor."

As if to prove her ownership of Dante, Albania found herself closest to him within this curious assortment of countries. It was her prison cemeteries that seemed assembled according to the Dantesque model. Prisoners whose death had transpired during their sentence rotted in these cemeteries. According to Albanian law, these corpses had to complete the years left in their sentences on prison grounds. Only after the corpses had served their time could they be reclaimed by their families.

Whereas in Dante's hell souls pay for the sins of the flesh, in Albanian cemeteries bodies bear the sins of the soul. Those serving life sentences would rot in prison grounds endlessly. Prisoners who were executed suffered a worse fate—they had no graves. There was no way to reclaim these bodies, since even the prisoners did not know to which random riverbank or deserted field they had been taken to be executed.

The Divine Comedy is the only work of literature in the world that simultaneously, and with the same intensity, reflected both the darkness and the light of communist Albania.

I would like to pose the question raised by Eugenio Montale during a Dante celebration: "What kind of significance does Dante's work hold for today's poets?" Different poets of the world have responded to this question differently, depending on their own "state." Naturally, Dante Alighieri always remains significant, but there are times when he doubles or triples in size.

The twentieth century was one such moment. At a point when it seemed as though Dante had reached the acme of glory and could go no further, communism swept through the world and Dante tripled in import.

With the narrative of a lonely journey into the land of the dead, he showed his brethren poets, whether they were Russian, Albanian, Baltic, or Chinese, that the natural state of the great writer is precisely this one—to be a traveler alive among the dead. He watched lifeless kingdoms, murderers, withered rice fields, and storms unfold in front of him. Monsters and dangers surrounded the writer, but he had the upper hand: he was alive, and they were not. Virgil's words, "do not fear the dead storm," are the poet's salvation. The whole essence of the "state" and, as a result, of fate, is encompassed in this formula.

Our conversation about Dante would be incomplete without remembering Beatrice. Dante wanted it to be this way. In fact, he took measures in order to ensure that it would be so, and we can only respond: let your will be done!

It is assumed that Dante wrote his poem cathedral in order to shelter Beatrice Portinari. Unlike any other edifice, this one began from the rafters, with paradise, and then descended to the bottom, into the cesspool. The poet desired that we picture Beatrice in the clouds, next to St. Mary. At the same time, Dante remembers her and even seeks news of her in the inferno.

The streets of today's Ravenna or Florence still resemble those of the past, and, along with the vulgar Italian, gave Dante their daily chronicles. From the language and the noisiness, he fashioned his divine poem. Despite the frowns of snobs like Alphonse de Lamartine, those streets and side streets, along with the Italian language, the fading lights, and the prostitutes under the rain, are intertwined with the poet.

Imagine a conversation in today's Italian streets between a prostitute and her client, one of those men who enjoy a postcoital cigarette: "You sound foreign . . . Ah, you are from Albania? I have never met any Albanians. What is your name? Beatrice. Beatrice? Do you have names like this one in your country or is this a nickname you assumed here . . . No, Beatrice is my real name! It is often used in Albania. Do you know with whom this name is associated here among the Italians? Of course, with Dante's Beatrice. Aha, so you know of the book. Of course I know it. I studied it in school."

This imaginary dialogue is not meant to create some sort of symbolic tie between the prostitute and Beatrice Portinari in order to lower the latter from the high, celestial place where Dante initially placed her. The first Beatrice of Dante's paradise and the Beatrice of the dark side streets of Milan, just as Jesus's two Marys, do not interfere with each other. One lives in the light and the other in the shadows.

Albanian women by the name of Beatrice, rare at the beginning of the century and increasingly frequent during the '30s, especially during the unification with Italy, are a result of the sense of belonging between Albania and Dante Alighieri. Names are difficult to dig up in the baptismal books of Albanian churches, the majority of which were demolished anyway. Instead, we can find records in the offices of civil affairs, where Christian and Muslim Beatrices were frequent.

Their chronicle would be incomplete if we did not also search for them in the lists kept in both countries' police stations, particularly among the names of those who have drowned while trying to cross the ocean in order to become Italian prostitutes.

Beatrices occasionally come up in the few memorial plaques that can be found in the seaside Albanian towns from which many small boats took off never to return again. Beatrice Kodheli, Beatrice Marku, Beatrice Brahimi, Beatrice X . . .

In these plaques we find touching words such as "let your soul find light in paradise, wherever you are." And it is precisely in paradise that we'll conclude this short history of Albania and Dante Alighieri.

(2005)

HAMLET,
THE DIFFICULT PRINCE

IT IS EASY TO SAY that Shakespeare's *Hamlet* is a universal work. In fact, one can confidently call it the most universal work in world literature. Much harder, though, is to ascertain whether such a characterization is a form of praise or an insult.

Invoking the word "universal" suggests that the greatest possible number of readers need to know *Hamlet*, and, therefore, that this work should aspire to be accessible to all. Familiarity and accessibility do not necessarily lessen a work's artistic merit. Universality in this case has less to do with the text's digestibility and more to do with a kind of rapport established with the work. Hamlet, both the play and the character, establish a close understanding with everyone.

In actuality, Hamlet's relations to the public can only be difficult, if not outright impossible. He remains unchanged, while the centuries are many and varied.

Across the stage on which the simplest and most complex act in the world will be played out, a story of murder, people come and take their place in succession, one after another. Northern and southern, white and black, Jews, Muslims, Christians, Buddhists, and atheists.

They are always there, this endless group of people whose presence only emphasizes Hamlet's own loneliness.

Everyone seeks something in *Hamlet*, and finds a small part of it only to lose it again on the spot. In their shock and awe, the audience loses what enchanted them and leaves it behind for another generation to rediscover it and then lose it yet again—and so the story continues indefinitely.

This doomed cycle is even more unforgiving toward those of us who love Prince Hamlet. We love him and are on his side when he blunders, because he resembles us. He is ours, of the same clan— deeply and mysteriously so. We identify with him, and here begins our misunderstanding. He is our portrait and yet does not obey us. He is a rogue reflection that brings out what we so carefully keep hidden. We want him to look pale and thoughtful, wrapped up in a prince's cape, and instead he stupidly revolves around the stage, shouting in his wooden clogs and socks. We can barely hold back our disapproval. Not like this, not like this! While our patience wanes and the misunderstanding deepens, we begin to consider the disrupted balance of *Hamlet* that Coleridge speaks about.

Calling *Hamlet* "universal" reveals more about ourselves than it does about *Hamlet*. With the exception of the Bible, no other book has been researched as strenuously as the drama of the prince seeking revenge. Scene after scene and line after line, *Hamlet* has been read and interpreted by hundreds, if not thousands, of researchers. Yet this analysis, instead of clarifying matters, has made things more opaque.

However contradictory it may seem, universality is tied to a text's mysteriousness. What we cannot determine in the case of *Hamlet* is whether the mystery makes the story universal or vice versa. Over the course of four centuries speculations about *Hamlet* have continued to surface. Most of them have dealt with the question of whether the events we see on stage are masking a different, possibly greater, darkness. Is what we have here a classic blood feud, or is it a crime disguised as revenge?

To this day, as these lines are written, Italian and Albanian criminals continue to confound judges by blurring the distinctions between these two crimes.

Haphazardly, we have arrived at the core of the theater itself: the masks and what is hidden behind them. We are dealing, as it were, with the eternal form, which, according to Plato, never shows itself—it merely sends out pale reflections of itself into our world.

As it happens when contemplating mysterious events of the past, we feel compelled to return to the place where everything originated—to the centuries-old stones, now polished by the wind, and to the grim limescale. In the case of *Hamlet*, we would need to go back to the Jutland flatland, a hinterland in the north of Denmark, near the sand dunes and northern frost. We would find no kings or princes or trumpets. What we would find are two brothers, Horvendill and Feng, both governing together. A woman, Horvendill's wife, stands between them. There is also the couple's only son, Amlet or Amleth. Finally, there is the specter of Horvendill, which, according to Coleridge, represents the interference from the netherworld sent in order to disturb the balance of the present.

One of the leaders, Horvendill, dies unexpectedly. Shortly after his death, his wife marries his brother, Feng. As though this were not enough to shock Amleth, the Prince begins to be haunted by Horvendill's ghost. The ghost announces that he has not died from a snakebite, as it is said, but that he was killed by his brother, Feng, and needs his son to avenge him. Amleth promises to do so and keeps the covenant.

From the beginning of the story, we feel that we have carried out our first sin. It is an original sin, *felix culpa*, which was born thanks to the art of storytelling. Because precisely in telling the story, we have changed something.

The trigger for this has not been a twisted artistic vein. It is simply the powerful reach of Shakespeare, who extended his influence not only on his contemporaries and on those who came after him, but also colored our view of earlier times. And so instead of the chronicles influencing our reading of Shakespeare, it is Shakespeare's influence that unsettles the chronicles.

From the start, we have fallen captive to a tyrannical Englishman. No ghost of Horvendill appears in the ancient Danish chronicle. And this is because there is no murder mystery. In Saxo's chronicle, Feng kills his brother openly, in the middle of a feast. Since there is no intrigue, there is no need for a phantom.

Can it be said, then, that from a lifeless mineral, a trivial piece of quartz, Shakespeare created precious jewels with little relation to the old chronicle?

Admiration for the playwright tempts us to agree, and to say that the ability to take an ordinary grain of sand and turn it into a pearl is the mark of a genius.

The pre-Shakespearean variant about the two brothers governing somewhere in Jutland is a simple one. During a banquet, the younger brother, Feng, brutally murders his older brother. Feng claims to have done so due to his brother's great severity with his sister-in-law. Shortly thereafter, the recently widowed woman, Gerutha, marries her husband's murderer. The hasty wedding leads the son, Hamlethus, to suspect a premeditated murder in which his mother may also have been involved. To avenge the blood of his father, he pretends to be deranged.

But is this all as simple as it seems? Is it complicated enough to scare us? Or is our fear a form of punishment inflicted on us because we dared dig where we do not belong, among the obscurities of life's relationship with art?

After all, we have a murder narrated in two ways: one by history and one by art. Sometimes the two seem very close, like twins, and sometimes they are entirely remote from each other. In one variant, there is a sensational murder, cruelly executed in the open by a killer whose cause is secret and vague. In the other variant, both the murderer and his motives are insidious and secret, and the story's spokesman is not of our world. And here is where everything gets complicated.

This factual story occurred four centuries before Shakespeare, according to testimony given by Saxo Grammaticus, the famous chronicler from Denmark. But, according to the ancient Icelandic sagas on which Saxo is known to have relied, the story is much older. Situated near the second century, the story of Hamlet is not that far from that of Christ. It is certainly much closer to ancient Greek theater than it is to the Globe Theatre of London, where it appeared for the first time on that holy night for art, on June 26, 1602.

If Homer was writing, as is believed, four centuries after the Trojan War, then the time that separated Shakespeare from his *Hamlet* is nearly four times as long. A very long time to justify a great deal.

Doubts about the figure of Hamlet, the boy prince who seeks to avenge his treacherously killed father, originated with the first appearance of the drama in London's famous Globe Theatre.

In the noisy edifice of the theater, the viewers, whether lords or ladies dainty in their lodges, sellers of vegetables, cads, or potential killers would have viewed Hamlet with suspicion. Many conjectures, at times forgotten as soon as they arose, accompanied *Hamlet*'s journey around the world. This is related to the genesis of theater—speculation and audience's suspicion is at the genre's very inception.

It is likely that the controversial marriage between the widow of Horvendill and his brother, Feng, pushed the unknown rhapsodist to compose his ballad. It was not every day that a woman married her brother-in-law when she had so recently shed tears for her late husband's death.

This story would not have looked the same had it happened a few thousand miles farther south, in the distant Balkans. In some parts of the peninsula, like among the Jews of old, it was common for one brother to sleep with the wife of his dead brother.

The well-known Albanian writer Faik Konica, friend of Apollinaire's, writes a critical rebuke in the early twentieth century against another prominent Albanian poet who had fallen prey to this custom, which Konica deems barbaric. As this case testifies, the custom continued in the Balkans as late as the nineteenth century.

However, we are not in the southern peninsula. We are far away in the North, where this marriage inspired suspicions significant enough to awaken a ghost. In other words, *Hamlet* could only have been born in the North. But we would be mistaken if we concluded that the South is somehow non-Hamletian. Hamlet's early brother, Orestes, experienced a similar drama on Greek lands.

Locating *Hamlet's* origin is not so simple. Among the myriad research studies, it is difficult to come across a genuine account of its beginnings. All research stops at Saxo's chronicle, and things go dark if we reach back further. Given this, it is natural for us to view *Hamlet* as an indication that despite some variants, the story has remained the same throughout time. We start from Shakespeare's rewriting, move on to Saxo, and conclude that there must have been a third chronicle that both resembles the previous two and does not look like either of them.

Let's go back to the old image of a dark night in the north, when the rhapsodist, after mourning, hears the wedding music from afar and is moved to sing of his burdens. He probably raised questions about the hasty marriage and the sudden death that had just taken place in the castle, but a ballad with this subject matter is probably not incendiary enough to catch on. Medieval ballads require something else. And so, death is summoned to the stage. Horvendill's death is a murder, a cruel one that occurs right in the midst of a celebration. What was once subtly implied is now rudely voiced by Saxo: the queen not only remarried in a hurry, but she also took her husband's killer. This variant makes for good tabloid journalism, but not for good art.

When Shakespeare and Thomas Kyd decided to write *Hamlet*, they likely realized the difficulties of making art out of this center-stage murder immediately. The first thing they must have decided to do was to displace the murder so that, until the phantom returns to tell the story, it happens in fog and complete silence.

The three variants thus provide three different tableaux. First, the dark northern night, wedding music, and a ballad imbued with forebodings. The second tableau, Saxo's, is quite the opposite: a feast, wine, toasts, knives in belts, women, and suddenly, like a wild beast, Feng lashes out and kills his brother. The third tableau, Shakespeare's, is quite different. Midnight in the castle walls in Elsinore, anguish, and the ghost.

All three paintings, no matter how different they seem, are connected by a thread of darkness. In the first picture, the oldest one, the darkness, although temporary, is everywhere. It also lurks in the second picture, despite the bright lights of the feast. What is this murderous frenzy? Feng's words, uttered in rage, make no sense. He calls his brother a tyrant, but whom was it that his brother was subjugating? The country, or perhaps the queen? Both, I believe. Suspicion always comes easily, and here it runs like the wind.

In the third variant by Shakespeare, an entire country, Denmark, awaits the emergence of the ghost in a crisis of anxiety. "Who's there?" "Nay, answer me: stand, and unfold yourself." These are the first two lines of *Hamlet*, the words of two guards on the walls of Elsinore castle. Burdened by the expectation of something horrible, the two guards are ready to mistake one other for a ghost. The statement demands an explanation, a discovery, the emergence of the hidden face—in short, a show.

In his Albanian translation, Fan Noli has chosen something akin to "show yourself." And, since in Albanian a spectacle is also called a "show," the guard's words in Fan Noli's Albanian read something like: "Appear, become theatricalized!"

The shadow of doubt that has first befallen Horvendill's wife quickly densifies. Inevitably, it darkens the circle of courtesans, then Hamlet's fiancée, the ghost, and finally lands grimly on Hamlet himself.

Suspicions and speculations rush to envelop everything. Even other works by the playwright are subject to this questioning. Shakespeare's sonnets undergo an unprecedented autopsy to reveal their hidden meaning, especially those related to homosexuality. The inquisitive eyes then turn to his sonnets; after them, nothing remains except the final stronghold, the author's biography. After this wreckage, when we think there can be no further desolation, comes the unbelievable: the skeptics deny Shakespeare's existence altogether.

Thus is created a dark ocean on whose banks Shakespeare scholars roam day and night. Among the hordes of readers, who are hard to define as either perverse, funny, or sad, there are also detractors. Most are insignificant and forgotten, but, here and there, big and clever names add to the chaos. The Spaniard Madariaga Salvador and the Russian Leo Tolstoy, for example, began their attacks against *Hamlet* in order to finish them against Shakespeare.

Shakespearean mayhem is to some extent reminiscent of another mess, that of Greek mythology. Its dark turbulence, within which characters and their motives surface chaotically, Oedipus, Ulysses, Prometheus, Philoctetus, Agamemnon, Ajax, and Clytemnestra among them, covers not only the Greeks but the whole world.

It is not easy to approach the Shakespearean plane. There are thousands of books, studies, surveys, and retorts, so it is natural to ask ourselves why we are impertinent enough to believe that we will say a single word that has not yet been said. We can only justify our presence by answering that we are human, and that Hamlet is, after all, a man, a member of our same race.

However, like all pathetic words, this justification is inadequate.

The author of these lines has pushed off the impetus to write this essay on *Hamlet* for over ten years.

Linking the Balkans and Hamlet via Konica's chronicle of the prominent Albanian Frashëri house, which also witnessed the marriage of a woman and her brother-in-law, seems a flimsy choice. Perhaps one could instead grab ahold of the mention of Illyria, today's Albania, in the beginning of *An Age of Kings*. But by using this criterion, Italy could lay claim to about a quarter of Shakespeare's work.

The Albanian blood feud makes for a more substantial connection, especially given that the original title of the drama was *The Revenge of Hamlet, Prince of Denmark*. Blood vengeance, though, was being overly used not only as the subject of Albanian literature, but also as a means of making Albania seem exotic, and, due to new prohibitive trends that pushed back against this, the relationship between *Hamlet* and the blood code went unmentioned for centuries. A stranger, Cyrus Sulzberger of *The New York Times*, announced this kinship in an early report in 1938. Sulzberger began by stating that it would have been more natural for Shakespeare to have set *Hamlet* rather than *An Age of Kings* in Illyria, the Albania of today.

The journalist hints that he could sense the atmosphere of Hamlet's tragedy both in the royal court and in Albanian life. Sulzberger's account rings true. King Zog I, as a true Albanian, was caught up in half a dozen stories of "blood." In his court, among his sisters and courtiers, roamed a boy nephew whose father had been killed, according to rumors, by his uncle-king. It is likely that through the secret service, the reporter was familiar with the intrigues of the court. He might have known, for example, that the king had summoned the orphaned nephew, Prince Tatin, newly arrived from Vienna for the burial of his father, and told him that the murder of his father was "man's business" and he would understand when he grew up. A Ferrari brought especially from Italy so that the boy could raise dust in the only boulevard of Tirana was even more effective than the words of the king at consoling Tatin's grief.

Sulzberger might have known even deeper things. For instance, he might have known that Ceno Bey Kryeziu, the father of the murdered man, a known Anglophone, and a rival of the king, intended to lift Albania out of the Italian and German influence by developing ties with the British in their stead.

The American journalist was, understandably, extremely cautious. In 1938, blood vengeance raged on in Albania, feeding the blacklists of daily newspapers. Along the unpaved roads of the country, one could see men whose black signs indicated their being in the midst of a blood vengeance.

For obvious reasons, Sulzberger's report was not known in Albania. The Albanian ambassador in Washington, Faik Konica, who was castigated for taking his dead brother's wife as his own, would likely have understood. He was known as the most erudite person in Albania and knew *Hamlet* better than anyone. He was, among other things, a manic-depressive who, if we are to believe Apollinaire, did not travel to Albania for fear that King Zog might poison him. Konica, therefore, would be in a position to understand better than anyone just how dangerous the US journalist's report was, and likely did everything he could to ensure that it went unnoticed.

The report of Sulzberger, who granted the Albanians a distant cousin in the north, did not reach Albanians until sixty years later, at the end of the century, when communism fell.

Hamlet has been read and staged in Albania, without interruption, throughout the entire twentieth century. But the somber Danish prince was also revisited under different circumstances in 1999, in Pristina.

It was November. For some time, since the bombings by NATO, Yugoslavia had been on her knees. Kosovo was free. Week after week, day after day, life was resuming. Newspapers came out again, cafés were whizzing with noise, and the theater of Pristina was preparing for its first free premiere.

This premiere's posters evoked elation, astonishment, and eventually fear and gloomy speculation.

The staging of *Hamlet* was, as it always is, rife with controversies. But this time, these polemics were not delineated by the stage. *Hamlet*'s boundaries grew slippery as a result of the political and military mess closing out the century: the war in the Balkans. All major governing bodies had participated; the entire world had watched and weighed in.

"Where did the Albanians find the time to prepare *Hamlet*?" "And why had they chosen *Hamlet*?"

The answer came quickly. It was murmured at first and then echoed in Belgrade newspapers, the radio, and the TV: the Pristina theater's choice of production was not a coincidence; it revealed a program of revenge to be exacted against the Serbian nation.

It was now Albanians' centuries-old enemies, the Serbs, who were linking the *Kanun* with Hamlet. According to the Serbians, the horrible Albanian blood vengeance had found its emblem in Shakespeare's drama.

Prince Hamlet, the Albanians' northern cousin who normally flattered Balkan pride, was now turning against them.

The night of the premiere, the theater of Pristina was full. The gloomy Albanians and uncomfortable Serbs had taken their places in the hall. There were also senior officials of the UN, the Council of Europe, officers of NATO, representatives of Amnesty International, the OSCE, the World Bank, members of every NGO possible, and finally, undercover agents from all types of foreign intelligence.

The best-known tragedy, staged for four consecutive centuries by millions of people and researched by thousands of specialists, was undergoing its strangest interpretation. In every part of the text, in the chosen décor, in the actors' tone, in short, in every detail, hidden undertones were sought. The audience was especially alert to signs of encoded meanings in the play's most mysterious parts, such as the pantomimes. The ghost might be very likely to order an entire nation to retaliate against a country that owed blood.

We can safely assume that the majority of reviews written about the show did not end up in the press but in secret archives, where, presumably, they never saw the light of day again.

After the unparalleled paroxysm that took place in the Pristina theater hall in 1999, let us turn to a controversy that was fixated upon by Shakespearean scholars. This discussion deals with Hamlet's wavering prior to avenging his father, a moment of uncertainty some think was overly prolonged and others consider much too brief. Some think that Hamlet's indecision is indicative of his noble nature, and others disagree. Goethe famously wrote that Hamlet collapsed under a burden that he could neither cast away nor carry; a statement that became the first party's motto. The other camp, which included the *Hamlet* translator, the legendary Bishop Fan Noli, insisted that Hamlet was not only unswerving, but also carried out so much death within a short period of time that he might qualify as an outright serial killer.

According to calculations made by Baron Tomasi di Lampedusa, who as a Sicilian was sensitive to the timeline of the feud, the play unfolds over the course of about four months, between March and June, of which only seven or eight days are played out on the stage. During this time, one after the other, Hamlet sends to their grave Polonius, Laertes, Ophelia's father, her brother, two older friends, Guildenstern and Rosencrantz, who are sent to certain death, and, finally, his uncle.

The dilemma surrounding Hamlet's uncertainty is naturally bound up with the question of whether what the ghost says is true. The first to suspect the ghost's veracity is Hamlet himself. For weeks, Hamlet attempts to find evidence that supports the ghost's account, beginning with the famous pantomime and turning to the show-trap *The Death of Gonzago*.

To doubt the ghost means to question Claudius's guilt, and thereby necessitates that we seek another potential killer. Hamlet's uncertainty is thus essential from the first act of the drama. Hamlet, like Oedipus, is not afraid to go toward the black hole itself, if there is one.

What, then, happened in Elsinore on that day in March when King Hamlet was found dead?

From the moment it happened, the office of the royal court announced a well-known story that has been repeated dozens of times in royal and presidential palaces throughout time. King Hamlet, Prince Hamlet's father, was bitten by a snake while he slept in the garden. This explanation is somewhat surprising considering that the event occurs in cold Elsinore, where poisonous snakes are rarely seen, let alone known to have poisoned anybody, particularly a king.

The other testimony, given by the ghost—in other words, the true testimony of what actually happened—is much less surprising. The ghost also blames poison, but, according to him, it was not a snake that killed the king: it was his brother, who poured poison into his ear!

This murder is so unusual that many are certain that it was just a euphemism for something else. According to them, the murderer leaned over his sleeping brother not to pour poison into the king's ear, but to whisper some horrible news: a threatening royal secret so powerful that the king died on the spot from a stroke.

Like any sudden death in a royal palace, the death of King Hamlet is accompanied by curiosities and mundane gossip, some of which is repeated by the ghost itself. The ghost, for example, admits that he was murdered after having sinned, implying that he was murdered in his sleep after having sex (with the queen, no doubt . . . or with someone else, which would not have been so unusual, especially for a king).

However, these whispers do not point decisively incriminating fingers.

We are always moving blindly inside the fortress that is Shakespearean drama. We know of some deceit regarding the death of a king. We learn that there was no snake, but poison handled by a murderous hand. Later, through a pantomime and a show-trap, we realize that the murderer has been revealed. In a monologue, Claudius, nestled in a corner of the stage, admits to the crime and puts everything to rest.

However, if there's anything in this world that does not fade easily, it is suspicion. It may slow down, become sleepy, and seem to have frozen like a snake in the winter, but it always remains. Somewhere between its slumber and hibernation, it quickens and comes to life, more disturbing than ever before.

In this case, like in most, our suspicious eyes turn to the woman. To suspect a woman is always easy. Moreover, in this case, the sixteenth-century French chronicler François de Belleforest, who made Saxo Grammaticus's story well-known in England, speculated that Feng had relations with his sister-in-law even while Horvendill was alive. Besides, if it was she with whom Horvendill was copulating for the last time when the worst happened, how it is possible that she neither saw nor felt anything? Usually it is men who fall asleep immediately after lovemaking.

But the ghost comes out most directly in her defense. He gives his son a clear-cut order: come what may, do not harm your mother!

Seasoned skeptics are ready to turn on the ghost as well. The ghost does not come out quite so cleanly in this story. It seems to be completely beholden to a feeling of guilt so powerful that his wife's adultery does not seem like such a disaster!

These speculators, however, often withhold themselves. They give up, just as they did with the inscrutable character of the prince's fiancée, Ophelia, or with the famous pantomime scene, where they could not help but notice that something was wrong. They shrug their shoulders. They don't know why Shakespeare has used the name "Hamlet" for both the prince and his father. Perhaps he did so to uncover a shared guilt, a man with two consciences, and a murder that is, in fact, nothing more than a suicide? But these and other suggestions have not inspired much curiosity.

Are the skeptics perhaps tired of following this line of thought? Or did they undergo a sobering awakening that has to do with the old understanding between humanity and its major art forms?

Some believe that humanity has been on the wrong path for all of its existence. However, even if we believe that humanity has chosen the wrong road, it would be fair to say that if there ever was a plane in which mankind had not made significant mistakes, it was with great art. History knows of no genius of letters, painting, music, or philosophy who has been forgotten. There are often delays in validation, but never oblivion. And so, no matter how far the controversy over *Hamlet* lasted, eventually everyone remembered the old pact between humanity and its literary masterpieces.

This drama's artistic merit is untouchable. Whether the story of the ghost was true or false, whether the wife had betrayed her husband before or after his death, whether the uncle was innocent or guilty, whether Ophelia was genuine, and whether the half-mad, cynical Prince Hamlet was a murderer or a compassionate son, the tragedy that bears his name remains a masterpiece.

Macbeth, too, does not lose artistic ground when we examine the chronicle of Holinshed and learn that, after the murder of the famous King Duncan, the king's corpse was not found in his bedroom, as Shakespeare suggests, but instead in an irrigation canal a few miles from the castle.

Similar investigations spring up around *Hamlet*, in part because of an early variant of the drama, *Ur-Hamlet*, written by Thomas Kyd (or by both Shakespeare and Kyd together), which vanished, surprisingly, from plain sight.

Thomas Kyd was imprisoned for political reasons and tortured into denouncing his twenty-nine-year-old colleague and fellow genius Christopher Marlowe, author of the famous *Doctor Faustus*. Marlowe was then summoned by the secret police to testify. The episode culminated in Marlowe's death a few weeks later, on May 30, 1593, under very strange circumstances in a London tavern—a gloomy tale that is painfully reminiscent of Stalinism four centuries later.

In May 1993, when across the UK the four hundredth anniversary of Marlowe's murder was being commemorated, London newspapers were publishing, among other things, a chilling drawing that sought to reconstruct what had happened in the tavern of the widow Leni Bull, where a villainous Londoner had stabbed Marlowe in the eye during a brawl.

It was natural that the newspapers sought to deal with the tragic event's more enigmatic elements. The torn eye of the playwright, turned into a black hole, required an explanation. Many things about Marlowe and Kyd, the affidavits from the investigation, and the death of the latter in prison were discovered, along with another, significant piece of information: these deaths and the communist terror, they realized, were quite similar.

Communism had collapsed only two years earlier and its secrets had barely been uncovered. However, something was emerging in May 1993, and it was doing so precisely in London. This occurrence was eagerly awaited, especially by the people of Eastern Europe, like the author of this essay. As if not enough fog hovered over Shakespeare, a new group of doubters were coming from the former communist empire. We, who came from those regions, might not have understood many things, but we were especially gifted when it came to questions of wire-tapping and intrigue!

We automatically associate the trio composed of Shakespeare, Marlowe, and Kyd with the dreadful word "group." A liberal writers' group, the group of Leningrad, the Petöf of Budapest club, the group of Mark Ndoja in Tirana, and so on.

The intelligence services of communist countries had borrowed from each other the basic terror scheme when it came to the arts. In a small group that has to be completely paralyzed, the first victim is usually sacrificed openly. (Thomas Kyd, according to the old model.) The second victim, the most dangerous one, dies quickly but not openly, because he is too famous (Christopher Marlowe, in this case). This death supposedly happens in some dark corner.

The third (William Shakespeare), will be left to live, but he will be monitored. If he does not learn the dangers of his trade from the other two murders, surely he can be taken care of as well.

Of all three cases, the murkiest one is that of Shakespeare. The enigma of Marlowe has been discovered, albeit belatedly. The same goes for the sad story of Kyd. Regarding Shakespeare, the most famous of the three, we know very little.

Shakespeare must have been under continual observation. Our Eastern European experiences become all the more insistent in this case, especially now in the early twenty-first century, a time of growing confusion over the secret tabs countries keep on their writers. These archives, other than recording bitter truths of life, also shed light on the deeper truths of relationships between nations and their prominent writers. This discovery, apparently, need not belong to any one country. Because hardly any country can say that the surveillance of renowned writers was simply an administrative matter; it was a matter of repression. It appeared in dozens of forms; even the form of worship turned into scrutiny.

The fog surrounding Shakespeare is not so different from the one that envelops Hamlet.

Hamlet's adventurous leaps between languages and genres constitute a story in themselves. From a ballad after a wedding, it turns into an Icelandic saga, and then, a thousand years later, into Saxo's official chronicle, commissioned by the Bishop of Denmark. Afterward, changing languages again, there is a book by Belleforest, this time in French. A short time later, as though it were feeling nostalgic for its earlier Icelandic incarnations, the poem turns into a drama by the Englishman Thomas Kyd.

We've only got a few small fragments left from this drama. They speak of the relationship between Hamlet and his mother, or rather, with their common plot, and prove just how suitable Hamlet's tale has been for the creation of its endless variants.

Meanwhile, Shakespeare's variant, the glorious creation that cut through all others, emerged on the stage. There could be no other Hamlet.

Hamlet was given a new life. We are not speaking of yet another iteration of Hamlet that sprung from his pilgrimage across different languages of the world. Nor are we referring to the poems, trials, films, portraits, studies, and controversies dedicated to the pale prince. This is an introduction to life in the true sense of the word. Hamlet has done something that rarely happens to artistic characters: he has crossed the threshold that separates art from life. As if in a nightmare, he left the world over 1,800 years ago in order to be summoned back by Shakespeare. Now his name, his image, is used by people naturally, as though he were one of them.

It is hard for him, but perhaps it is even more difficult for us.

He is distant, threatening, and cold; like any clone who returns from a long exile, from artificiality, from art. Our world is no less cool or ruthless with him. He must endure its messiness and infinite cynicism. He appears before us as if he were in court, ready to be judged and to pass judgment on us rigorously, dispassionately.

You love me, deny me, and suspect me. I also love, deny, and suspect you.

As if we were browsing through childhood pictures of a relative changed by glory, wealth, or crime, so we return to the place where Hamlet's perplexing beginnings occurred.

In the Jutland wasteland where news takes weeks to arrive, everything is dull and sluggish except for hatred. Only hatred can blossom in the gloom of Jutland.

Sand crunches under the natives' feet and cracks between their teeth when they speak, increasing their despair. On the sand have stepped the boots of the two brothers who led the provincial government, Horvendill and Feng. This environment witnessed the incident that at times we seem to know too much about, and at other times not nearly enough.

There was hatred, of course, dry, insoluble, and as thick as the sand. There was incest and despair. There was a sudden death and then a rushed wedding, with sad music and words. Grim whispers and gritty sand. The event encompasses all the miserliness of death.

When T. S. Eliot expressed the seemingly surprising opinion that *Hamlet* transcended the possibilities of Shakespeare, he truly meant to say that *Hamlet* transcended every artistic possibility. We might call it an impossible drama.

This is a likely explanation for the fever of allegations that has always surrounded *Hamlet*.

The skepticism never fully stopped, but it did undergo a radical shift and turned against Shakespeare himself. What little and conflicting information we have on the playwright's life began to be plastered on all of his publications. The public fixated, too, on supplementing the playwright's scant biography with the help of cryptography, spiritualism, or even the mask placed on Shakespeare's grave after his death. That cold mask of copper, which has completely covered Shakespeare's true face, proves that he was a marked man.

The well-known affirmation that Shakespeare was the greatest writer in the world is often voiced, almost trivially, both in England and abroad. There have been attempts to completely exile his prized treasure from England, giving the author a Flemish identity, or that of an Arab, or of who knows what else. Even as I write this, in the fall of 2005, someone has just published a book titled *The Truth Will Out*, which is meant to prove that the author of the famous plays was a distinguished diplomat of royal lineage who had a career in Austria, Italy, France, and Denmark before he was imprisoned. Obviously, nearly every claimant to the Shakespearean crown is a blue-blooded dignitary—some even contest that the Bard was none other than Queen Elizabeth I of England! At times, this seems a prank that the world wants to play on the writer, who spent his life describing warring monarchs and princes, some legitimate and some looking to cheat others out of the crown. Now Shakespeare, the greatest, most legitimate prince of art, has his own crown threatened by impostors.

Is this a paradox? The word "paradox" is usually invoked too hastily. This is something else. For each country, it seems, including one as covetous as the UK, either too great an honor or too great a shame is disturbing. The temptation to find a phenomenon that compares to the power of geniuses is a common one. Meteors, high mountains, hurricanes, cathedrals, earthquakes, and storms are a few examples. Some geniuses, like Dante Alighieri, are lucky to be compared to a cathedral. Others, like Shakespeare, have not had the same luck and are compared to a forest in the midst of a storm. Some have likened him to an earthquake. Despite the frustration these often reductionist comparisons occasion, comparing Shakespeare to a great disturbance makes great sense.

Shakespeare disrupts our sleep. He distorts everything. This is why there are seasons, and perhaps whole eras, when he becomes to our eyes an intolerable conqueror and we demand his fall.

No matter if they were fitting, inappropriate, rational, or driven by a desire to love *Hamlet* more deeply, the uncertainties surrounding this play should have either been completely clarified or faded significantly. The opposite happened. Precisely in the twentieth century, at a time when human knowledge had advanced enough that it could analyze the teeth of an Egyptian mummy and determine whether the pharaoh had eaten honey on his last morning, *Hamlet* fell under a complete fog. Questions about what happened between Hamlet, his father, his mother, and his uncle in the cold of Jutland began to swell in a frightening way, and suspicions prevailed again.

In November 1917, when John Dover Wilson read an article on *Hamlet* as he sat in a train bound for Sunderland, his entire life changed direction. The experience was so powerful that it made him, an inspector dealing with the issue of education in the army, leave everything and become the largest British specialist on Shakespeare. His subsequent book *What Happens in Hamlet*, published by Cambridge University Press in 1935, stirred many waters, but by then the storm had already been brewing.

Why precisely did this storm climax in the twentieth century? As with many questions surrounding *Hamlet*, there was no clear-cut answer. It was doubtlessly the cruelest century after the birth of Christ. Genocide was performed not only more cruelly than ever, but also often covered up so that it remained in the dark for years. This was a century of crime, madness, and hypocrisy. So much so, that *Hamlet* reflects its face better than any other drama.

According to C. Jon Delogu's interpretation, the deadly poison that King Hamlet's brother poured into his ear was nothing more than bad news. We, the people of the twentieth and twenty-first centuries, finding ourselves in front of the radio and television every day, are a sleeping King Hamlet. Gloomy and disturbing news, as threatening as poison, is poured into our ears incessantly.

We are under constant pressure. All kinds of ghosts appear to give us new orders. Karl Marx, Freud, St. Augustine, anti-Semitism, terrorism. We listen, but then falter and suspect that perhaps neither the information nor the orders given have been correct.

There comes an unbearable moment when, as if in a bad dream, Hamlet takes on our image. We remember the angry Stalin interrupting Shostakovich's opera *Lady Macbeth of Mtsensk*, Mao Zedong doing the same at a theater in Beijing, and Enver Hoxha halting a performance in a theater in Tirana. There always comes a moment in the life of a communist regime when the tyrant stands and, like Hamlet's uncle, cries out: stop the game, turn on the lights! This happens not only with tyrants. In the twentieth century, Hamlet was an apt reflective surface for everyone, hence the seemingly endless analytical scouring the character underwent.

Now our misgivings deepen, like the thick fog that enveloped *Hamlet* from the start. Both Queen Gertrude, the Prince's mother, and Ophelia, his fiancée, find themselves under investigation. Is the queen guilty in this story? If so, of what crime? At the very least, of breaking her mourning by marrying her brother-in-law so urgently. But she might be guilty of something worse. Did she commit matrimonial treason even earlier, when the king was still alive? Did she participate in his murder?

According to Belleforest's chronicle, she betrayed her husband while he lived. As for murderous collusion, the chronicler is silent. According to the ghost, Gertrude played no part in the murder, but she did desecrate the matrimonial bed. It is not clear, however, whether he means she desecrated their matrimonial bed while he still lived, or whether it is her new marriage that is the aberration.

The ghost of King Hamlet is not very clear, and we do not know whether he is all-knowing. At first glance, he seems to be, but he never mentions the wedding between the queen and the killer. This omission makes many suspect that when he speaks of betrayal, the ghost simply means adultery. If this is true, to our colossal surprise, the betrayed king does not seem particularly angry at his wife over something that would make others take up the axe of retribution.

Perhaps the king's overly liberal behavior is the result of a fault of his own. Maybe he knows himself to be guilty of a similar crime. But we will come back to this later.

The other woman, Ophelia, the embodiment of a million girls' sublime dream (the dream of being a princess, which withstood the downfall of monarchic systems), keeps us at a distance.

In Hamlet's ramblings, she is talked about as either a nun or a whore. Not only is her virginity mentioned, but there is some discussion that it may have been lost not to Hamlet but to someone else. And then there is her whole behavior. It is both compassionate and cold—a winter sun that does not provide any warmth.

Ophelia is an impossibility for herself, for Hamlet, and for us all. There is an unspoken guilt and a girlish sadness within her, which remains unexplored by scholars. In the kingdom of men, the world of millions of teenage girls is, regrettably, still ignored.

Everyone must negotiate a barrier in this tragedy, but the biggest obstacle lies between us and Hamlet. Even so, he is with whom we identify most closely. Our dispute with Hamlet hurts us the most. There comes a moment when it seems as though we will never understand one another. In our desperate attempt to reprimand him, somehow we manage a negligible victory. Instead of the madman who wanders around miserably, we get a prince with a black cape who does not lose his dignity even in moments of madness.

We cannot endure another Hamlet. We cannot bear his disturbed portrait, and much less his guilt. Like the ghost, like Queen Gertrude, like Ophelia, he carries a heavy burden. And witnessing his crime is the worst of all.

But let us return to 1917, to the train wagon where inspector John Dover Wilson is traveling to Sunderland.

*

It is the last year of World War I, and Northern Europe, just like the entire continent, is tired and sad. The army inspector, Wilson, continues his joyless journey in a cold train. A man of letters and a fan of Shakespeare, he tries to find the time to read a little between railway stations. One such time, while opening letters, he picks up an article by Walter Wilson Greg on the fog surrounding Hamlet. His shock is such that he instantly forgets the war, the fate of Europe, his office, and thinks of nothing but how to respond to the scholar.

That article, which Wilson reads several times while on the train, contains the "devil's charm." Wilson's first thought is to return it to where it came from, in other words, send it back to hell. In the telegram he sends to *The Modern Language Review*, along with a request for them to publish his reply, he insists repeatedly that Greg's article deserves hell. As Wilson argued for years, Greg's article raised a great, foundational question, which shook the whole edifice underlying *Hamlet* like an earthquake.

The famous pantomime in the third act, used to prove the guilt of the killer, is a genius effort that ventures into some of the darkest areas of the world.

Pantomime, a theater within a theater, comes automatically equipped with a magical ambiance. It has a dual nature. It exists in a mixed time that negotiates between reality and fantasy. Having tried to penetrate what our eye does not see, it serves as a kind of crystal that breaks through the laws of our world. The dull and dark pantomime in *Hamlet*, combined with the clarity of the mini-drama, reminds us of the dichotomy between knowing and not knowing—a true human torture.

This is what Shakespeare calls a "miching mallecho," a coinage that is partly English, partly Spanish, and partly sourced from vulgar ports; and which was translated into Albanian by Fan Noli as "machine villain." This "machine villain" is connected to the ghost. After all, it is his script. The phantom is not only King Hamlet's double, it is the thin membrane that separates the two kingdoms of this world: that of being and that of nothingness. Nobody wants to die, but we all do. Everyone wants to return from death, but no one does. In order to comfort us as we face this inevitability, nature created a plane of nonexistence: dreams. Those unsatisfied with mere dreams have summoned ghosts.

W. W. Greg does not deal with any of this. His is a single-minded focus. After expressing his surprise at having discovered something that went unnoticed for centuries, Greg unfolds the riddle. What he is uncovered has to do with Claudius's calm during the pantomime. The pantomime, though dull, is clear: a king is killed in his sleep by poison that was poured into his ear. To everyone's great surprise, Hamlet's uncle, the suspected murderer, is not particularly impressed by the pantomime. According to Greg, the alleged murderer does not stumble because he does not recognize the crime being played out. Greg believes that Hamlet's uncle is irritated by his nephew, especially for Prince Hamlet's anger at the queen's rushed wedding, which should have been spoken of quietly instead of echoed so publicly in this pantomime. In short, Claudius is unaffected by something that would shake every murderer: the reproduction of the crime scene, captured in a pantomime more faithfully than it could have been captured by anything else.

Consequently, according to Greg, either the ghost's story was untrue, or the ghost was invented by Hamlet himself. But what about the officers, the men who were there when Hamlet encountered the ghost? They might have witnessed the ghost, but nobody heard their words, answers Greg. In short, the pantomime calls into question the ghost and also Hamlet himself. Claudius is acquitted, and another killer must be found.

All of the drama's internal logic is disturbed. And yet, despite the mask that appears on Prince Hamlet's face, *Hamlet* the tragedy retains its integrity.

However, this does not prevent the deluge of speculations that Greg's discovery has occasioned. The ghost is merely Hamlet's hallucination. *The Death of Gonzago* is also a scenario he has concocted. The friends who saw the shadow were either under the collective influence, or, knowing Hamlet's paranoia, pretended to see things.

Suspicions now fall on the prince openly. Dr. Sigmund Freud, who was all too eager to partake of a banquet that seemed specially laid out for him, gets involved, but is surprisingly restrained in the end. Questions revolve around Hamlet's delay to kill Claudius. According to the Oedipus complex, this hesitation is natural. It is hard to retaliate against the man who killed one's father. The psychoanalyst Ernest Jones is more decisive. He proposes that Hamlet's fear of Claudius has to do with the fact that by murdering Claudius, he would also kill himself.

To compound matters, an old crime appears faintly, as though reflected in a foggy mirror. A crime that Shakespeare knows but remembers only in passing, like a half-forgotten history. The duel between King Hamlet and the neighboring Norwegian king is a dark stain on the king's conscience. The monarchs dueled for a piece of the other's kingdom and for each other's queen. King Hamlet, determined not to lose his land or his woman, wins the duel through trickery. The outcome, clearly, is more or less the tragedy *Hamlet*. The scene is nearly the same, as though it were an image in an old but very dusty mirror. The trickery and Queen Gertrude are present in both calamities, but all of this is so vague that even the reading, even the drama, does not attract attention.

In this case, the symmetry of crime related to *fatuum*, quite favored in the Greek theater, would not have been ignored by the irreverent author of *Hamlet* if he were not also writing another drama, *Macbeth*, which has at the center crime in all its fatality.

Hamlet and *Macbeth* do not outwardly resemble each other and are even less similar at their core. Macbeth carries out a crime to feed his hunger for power, whereas Hamlet interrupts this search for power in another. And since interrupting a crime is rarer than enabling its continuation, the model of the circuit breaker is the one viewed suspiciously.

As though in a fever, researchers rummaged through any available material in order to elucidate Hamlet's questionable behavior. They turned to the playwright's life story, which is powerful but short, and as might be expected, they focused on Shakespeare's relationship to his father. Researchers likely paused when they encountered the fact that John Shakespeare died in 1600 and *Hamlet* was written in 1601. Could William have had some parricidal impetus? Was he, unknowingly, a Hamlet?

Since the above suspicion led nowhere, scholars had to be satisfied with the tiny, mediocre thesis that grief over his father's death prompted Shakespeare to write *Hamlet*. But even this modest idea was not sustained for long, because it is hard to believe that the forty-year-old Shakespeare, the equivalent of a sixty-year-old today, would be so troubled by the death of his father that he would pen his most haunting drama as a result.

This conjecture, however, has at least originated a somewhat unexpected and beautiful idea: can we imagine a *Hamlet* written by Hamlet?

Ella Sharpe wrote that Hamlet is not Shakespeare, but rather who the poet would have been had he not written *Hamlet*. According to Sharpe, the play's characters are merely introjections issued and discarded by Shakespeare's psyche. In other words, the Hamletian being, in writing *Hamlet*, ceases to be Hamlet.

Although this reasoning seems circuitous, it gives rise to another, more tangible question: what would Hamlet make of his own drama? Indeed, during both the pantomime and the mini-drama, Hamlet occupies the role of a spectator. He is also the author of at least twelve lines added to the text of *The Death of Gonzago*, as well as the director and an indirect character of this play, since it deals with his own father's murder. Finally, he is both an art critic and an investigative chronicler who seeks to uncover crime through theater. In short, he sees his own figure on the scene.

Given all this, it is not at all surprising that in a theater hall where the drama is being staged, we would ask: is there a Hamlet in this hall?

The question has been a reasonable one from the first appearance of the drama on June 26, 1602, all the way to our time. In every manifestation of the drama, everywhere in the whole world, there have always been people in the hall thirsting for revenge. In short, there was always a Hamlet in the room, witnessing their own drama on the stage.

We are in the intermediate area between the author, the drama, and the spectator. In Shakespeare's time, this liminal area simmered with rage. In 1597 alone, nine killings took place during the show in the London theater. The wealthier spectators came to the theater accompanied by armed guards. The divide between the stage and the spectators was often breached. Blood vengeance constituted the core of the drama. When the theaters were closed due to the plague, the people of London, despite their boredom, enjoyed finally having some peace and quiet. When the theater reopened, they returned as though they were heading into an ambush.

The diversity of spectators, from the lowly bellhops to the lords in their lodges, was only surpassed by the variety of performances the actors played on stage. *Hamlet* presided over this race. To appear like Hamlet. To explain Hamlet. To change Hamlet. To reflect the true Hamlet. The startling variety in the stage décor and the choice of actors is dictated by this deep thirst for identification. The ghost of the murdered king has appeared on stage in everything from military clothes and pajamas to sneakers. Women did not escape the desperation to identify with the dark prince. As W. H. Auden loved to tell his students, the actress Sarah Bernhardt insisted so strongly that she identified with Hamlet that she was finally given the role of the prince, and during the show even broke her leg.

The expression by Ion Omesco, "Germany is Hamlet," remains famous to our day. This universal need to identify with *Hamlet* speaks to the play's colossal proportions. It is hard to believe, as psychoanalysts insist, that the key to *Hamlet*'s seductiveness is the repressed libido of the child and the Oedipus complex story. The answers to *Hamlet*'s mysteries should be sought elsewhere. Humanity keeps attending performances of *Hamlet* not as if they were headed for a psychoanalyst's couch, but as if they were witnessing a solemn mass of the arts.

Are there Hamlets in the hall? Are there Hamletians? Are there murderers in the crowd?

In the theater of Pristina, in November 1999, these questions were raised in a hurry— politically, even militarily. The questions were not directed at two or three people, or even a group of terrorists that might have infiltrated the theater; they were addressed to an entire population.

Just as the pantomimes in *Hamlet* were a theater performance within the theater, so *Hamlet* was a synecdoche for the theatrics of the Balkan conflict during the last year of the millennium. But while the play's pantomimes would prove one man's guilt for crimes committed in the past, *Hamlet* warned of future crimes that would be perpetrated on an entire people.

Are there Hamletians here?

When in 1938 the American Cyrus Sulzberger titled part of his book "Hamlet Among the People of the Eagle," he must have known that Hamlet was a renowned guest in the Balkans. This section might also be called: "Hamlet Among His Own," or "Hamlet Among Hamletian People." In the Albanian mountains, Hamlet really was among his own people. He had lived there for centuries prior to the arrival of *Hamlet*, Shakespeare, or even theater itself. The Albanians played the role of the Prince in their own way, but they always did so faithfully. They took their orders from a code more ruthless than the ghost, and carried out instructions that invariably led to their own deaths.

Jean Starobinski once said there is no need to seek something deeper than Oedipus because Oedipus is depth itself. Hamlet is the exact opposite. At each new level of depth, the end cracks open only to reveal yet more cavernous space.

The tireless Ernest Jones, in his *Hamlet and Oedipus*, cites the northern Celtic and Icelandic sagas among the sources of Hamlet's primordial myth. Having descended into Central Europe and the Balkans from the Vikings, Hamlet climbed back north, enriched by the peninsula's madness. Otto Luitpold Jiriczek, a well-known name in the Balkans, traces the Prince's roots in *Hamlet in Iran*. Another researcher, Charles Fries, speaks about an Indian Hamlet, while many others have traced Hamlet's origins to Roman and Greek sources of old. Needless to say, Oedipus is the perennial favorite, whereas Orestes is often overlooked. Psychoanalysts find the former captivating and the latter somewhat of a nuisance.

*

Incestuous relationships between siblings have reverberated among the Greek, Albanian, and South Slavic people until quite recently. Sibling incest flits about *Hamlet* apprehensively, as though there were not enough room for it among all the other major calamities. Enter a Finnish Hamlet named Kullervo, whose wife drowns herself out of desperation when she discovers she is married to her brother. Many scholars have toyed with the possibility of Hamlet and Ophelia's being brother and sister. Needless to say, poor Ophelia had to escape this incestuous image somehow.

Hamlet's tangible map—which spans Denmark, Norway, England, and Poland—is narrow in comparison with the tragedy's internal atlas—which covers nearly half the planet: the Roman, Byzantine, and Ottoman Empires, and the European centers and coasts.

According to Gilles Deleuze, literature invents nonexistent people. In the case of *Hamlet*, the word "invention" should be replaced by the term "discovery." *Hamlet* discovers centuries of vindictive avengers. Our world has always been full of them, but tragedy precipitated a leap via which Hamlets grew to become the majority and theirs became the ruling code. To capture this more simply, we can turn to an archipelago by the name of Gulag and to its population of zeks. Both the map and its residents were discovered by a Russian Columbus by the name of Solzhenitsyn in the second half of the twentieth century.

There have always been prisoners, deportations, and detention areas somewhere in the world, but there came a time in the history of the USSR when these areas sprawled to such an extent that they gave rise to a second map, becoming a state within a state. This space and its swelling boundaries turned into the true map of Russia. It not only became significant because of its extension and number of inhabitants, but also due to its mentality—its prevailing sense of anxiety and dread.

But let us return to our lineage of Hamlets.

There are areas in the south of Europe—Corsica, Sardinia, Sicily, Montenegro, Crete, and Albania—where at certain times and under certain circumstances, blood avengers constituted the ruling class. Via still unexplored processes, the dark magma of personal revenge grew into a civil and criminal constitution. This code lived in tandem with the state, its weight and authority not based on the police, courts, or prisons, but rather on public opinion. It sought to either defeat the government or to replace it altogether. This code is an exotic remnant of an old and universal phenomenon. Greek tragedy proves this widely, and even an earlier Homeric text describes a blood vengeance trial similar to those that still exist today in the Balkan Mountains.

Blood vengeance, which has turned into an identifying Albanian trait, resurfaced after the fall of communism and the half-century ban of the code it had imposed. Any discussion about the future of Albania includes mention of its *Kanun*. Meanwhile, two founding European countries, France and Italy, operate their blood codes in Corsica, Sardinia, and Sicily without a fuss.

In Saxo's chronicle, where the story of Hamlet takes up about forty pages, there are just two events that coincide with the Albanian *Kanun*. The first relates to the surprising pact between Horvendill, Hamlet's father, and the Norwegian King Koll moments before their duel. They promise to attend each other's funeral, no matter who wins. This unusual oath, so surprising it survives the telling and retelling of this tale, is mandatory in the Albanian code.

We have here a death within a death. The murderer finds himself among his enemies, those who grieve over his deed. Despite many attempted explanations, the need for the killer's presence remains opaque. Saxo, like many others, attributes this oath to an attempt to mitigate hatred within communities, but a murderer who walks among the funeral party is more likely to heighten animosity.

The murderer's presence causes a rift in the funerary rites. There is, on the one hand, the death of the victim, but there is also the future death of the killer, an impending ceremony that he sees in his victim's funeral, as though it were a hallucination.

Hamlet's outcry about mutilated rites comes out of his mouth as he thinks about the complex rites of marriage and death.

The second coincidence has to do with the king of England, Hamlet's host, friend, and father-in-law, who liked him so much after meeting him that he immediately gave him his daughter's hand in marriage. Everything goes wonderfully in this idyll, until the moment the king learns from Hamlet's own mouth that he has murdered his evil uncle, Feng. The news confounds the king. Unfortunately for Hamlet, his father-in-law was Feng's friend, and they had vowed to avenge each other's blood if one of them was murdered . . .

And now we land on the issue of the oath, the Albanian besa, a cornerstone of the *Kanun*. More precisely, we arrive at a discussion about an unjust besa that is binding and sacred nonetheless.

In 1938, when Cyrus Sulzberger identified the Hamletian tendencies of Albanian mountain-dwellers, he described a part of the population as blond, beautiful, and thin. They seemed to him to have emerged "right out of the House of Lords," a statement that made the above connection quite obvious. Hamlet's shadow must have been part of the appeal the local Albanians held for Sulzberger. Oddly, though, Sulzberger never reports having had a conversation with the Albanians. For an intellectually curious journalist, this seems like a missed opportunity.

At the time, disputes surrounding Hamlet and psychoanalysts' insistence on probing the Prince with their theories on the repressed libido or the Oedipus complex were at their height. It must have been amazing for Sulzberger, aware as he was of the confusion that hovered above this mysterious character, to exit a world of speculations about the darkness, ambiguity, and symbolism of the soul and enter a concrete world in which real people wander around and resemble the Danish avenger of blood. Sulzberger had Hamlet in front of him as an objective being, a completely external Amlethus, primal but epic in the true sense of the word. He could have even taken a picture of him with his camera.

Yet Sulzberger could not forge a relationship with him. Was it because the locals were unfriendly? Was it their custom to be reserved? This might have played a role, but the most important reason was probably something else. The American journalist must have felt that these blood avengers were "different" in the deepest sense of the word. They were doubly impossible to understand: they were "different" even among their own people. It was another population, similar to the one that Deleuze has in mind, when he talks about missing people.

In 1938, when Sulzberger visited Albania, blood seekers were everywhere. They followed their path silently, their ages varied, they moved with a serious look and free of the usual swagger. The code forbade blood seekers from expressing excitement at the prospect of killing. How could they be excited when their mission was bound up with their own death? They appeared in the streets like members of a sect, with their distinguishing mark of death, a black armband, sewn on their sleeves. If one of them had found themselves by chance in a theater where *Hamlet*, which was being shown in Albania at that time, was being played, the blood seeker would have found a new brother and a fellow blood seeker.

In Albanian, the word *gjaks*, or "blood seeker," comes from the root word "blood." The Albanians consider gjaks a neutral word that bears no relation to the word "murderer." The blood seeker is simply a person who deals in blood, much like a blacksmith works with metal. A blood seeker is not considered a murderer, he is just someone who must perform an obligation, like an executioner. Taking blood under the *Kanun* simply means to take a human life.

The black armband announces the blood seeker's fate every-where—on the street, walking by the court building, or even as he walks past policemen. And yet no one impedes the seeker of blood. Everyone accepts that he has received an order that cannot be questioned or avoided. Walking behind him is a protection stronger than the law: that of the *Kanun*.

This man is part of the population of blood seekers, who, as noted above, are a people within a people. However, unlike most minorities, these men belong to an elite.

The blood seekers and the blood givers are caught up in an exchange of blood, or are "in the blood." This is another expression that is completely neutral in Albanian. It shows an objective relationship, which, in this case, has to do with blood. One party must give and the other must take.

The whole situation is as clear and cold as a frozen winter day. No accompanying resentments, no questions, no efforts to convince the masses about who is right and who is not. The *Kanun* defined everything a thousand, two thousand years ago.

Despite this neutrality, the status of each party involved is akin to the two sides of the moon: the visible and invisible one. The population of the blood seekers is visible, while the other, which awaits the hit, lives a more shadowy life. This population bears no insignia on the sleeve, and it is unclear who the next victim will be.

However, this state of affairs is temporary. From the moment when the blood seeker performs his obligation, the situation is reversed. The blood seeker becomes "de-Hamletized," to use Ella

Sharpe's term. He passes on to the other side of the spectrum and awaits his own death in the shade. The demeanor of his whole clan changes. He crouches, waiting now that the wheels have turned and it is the other party's turn to seek the blood.

These receivers and givers of blood are born of abnormal conditions, and are therefore an abnormal population. They lead a life parallel to other laws and calendars and out of keeping with an ordinary conscience. Theirs is a tragic conscience.

We are naturally drawn to the essence of tragedy, which arises from just such tragic consciences. We have nearly distilled tragedy. Not only the funeral but the taking of the blood, the murder, resemble a murderous theater. Villages and whole regions serve as a ruthless jury, observing how every step of the event unfolds. They watch to ensure that the *Kanun* is honored. Did the blood seeker shout the mandatory formula before firing his gun? Or did he replace the phrase with unworthy obscenities? After the murder—was the body turned around? Was a rifle placed beside him, as is required by the *Kanun*? Has the murderer rushed to the Path of the Cross in the village to announce to the family that he killed X? Did he go to the funeral and sit quietly, without pride? He is less a man of flesh and blood, and more an actor reading lines from this ancient code.

In Albania, everyone remembers the assassination attempted of the future King Zog that occurred in front of parliament on February 23, 1924 by Beqir Valteri, who was avenging his uncle's blood. Because of a speech impediment, the assassin delayed in uttering the words required by the *Kanun*, "pass on greetings to my uncle," enabling the king to avoid the fatal bullet.

The theatricality of the funeral ceremony, especially the professional criers, an echo of the choir in the ancient theater, suggests that the townsfolk who attended funerals preferred the performance of pain to its real experience. This externalization of pain gave mourning a public dimension that, sooner or later, would lead back to the theater.

Unlike a funeral, which commences with death, theater typically ends with death. The theater of blood feuds presents yet another model: through the blood seeker, death is present not just at one end of tragedy but throughout the whole performance. These feuds are so performative that it is difficult to understand where death ends and their theater begins.

After the assassination attempt that took place on the steps of parliament, the bloody and pale future King Zog enters the parliament to give his anticipated speech. The assassin, after an exchange of fire with the guards, gives himself up in a state of delirium while singing patriotic songs. He makes vague and controversial declarations. He says he wants to save Albania from a tyrant and adds that he has to avenge his uncle's blood. According to article 887 of the *Kanun*, blood, whether royal or ordinary, has the same value once shed, so the assassin is cleared of all blame. He has done what Hamlet is accused of doing—he has masked a political murder with blood vengeance.

At the time of the assassination attempt, Albanian law had officially forbidden and yet continued to honor blood vengeance. The assassin placed his hopes in the public's opinion. The future king also preferred to view the attempted assassination as a cry for blood vengeance instead of as a sign of political unrest. So Beqir Valteri, who under different circumstances might have hung in the center of Tirana, was released.

The theater prevailed over national laws. According to article 950 of the *Kanun*, Beqir Valteri owed King Zog as much blood as he had claimed. He owed a wound, or a "half-blood."

The story was just one of hundreds of events, proving the triumph of the *Kanun* or its theatricality over everything else, even royal anger.

It has been said many times that the theater serves as a mirror for the world, as an "ars rotunda" that recalls the globe, sky, stars, hell, zodiac diagrams, and the final judgment. The aptly named Globe Theatre in London seemed to run according to this motto, and its inscription "Theatrum mundi" (world theater) revealed its vision.

The relationship between man and the theater seems as inevitable in deserted snowy mountains as it does in metropolitan centers. It is difficult to separate our assumptions, crimes, and great feats from the theater. The sensational statement, the killing that will be forever remembered, the rebellion, the coup—all of these have originated in the theater.

Back in 1997, when post-communist Albania was mired in tragic confusion, people, intoxicated by the television cameras that had come to witness this historic moment, did many stupid things in front of foreign reporters, even killing others as though they were on a stage. The confusion was famously captured by an Albanian teenager's response to someone's call for restraint: What are you saying? How can you ask for restraint when we haven't yet made the first headline on Euronews?!

The murders, fires, and even the overthrow of the state did not seem as horrendous to the teenager as the possibility that the reigning performativity of it all would fade away. Thirst for glory, a thirst that obscures reason, is powerfully present in Hamletism. Ur-Hamlet, Amleth, Amlod, and Amlethus are all marked by this vice of theater. Saxo's lines on the Danish prince's death confess Hamlet's performativity (Book 4, chapter 2): "So ended Amleth. Had fortune been as kind to him as nature, he would have equaled the gods in glory, and surpassed the labors of Hercules by his deeds of prowess. A plain in Jutland is to be found, famous for his name and burial-place." This inherent performativity that we can call the "internal Hamlet" can be very openly encountered where the prince naturally transcends the scene and acts like the "external Hamlet."

A meeting between a Balkan blood seeker intent on avenging his father's blood and Hamlet would be quite interesting. Understanding the connection between them is quite difficult. It is not easy to discern if the two are united by the same burden. Are they cynical people willingly committing murder, or are they fragile creatures who regret what they are about to do? Regarding the latter, the *Kanun* recognizes that someone may become sick at the sight of blood. This is not viewed as a weakness—the *Kanun* even gives instructions on what the blood vengeance seeker should do if this happens.

Blood seekers speak rarely. The black marks on fellow seekers' sleeves are one of the only things that can compel them to exchange two words with others. The will-be killers might discuss the road and the inn where they are staying, or the region where they come from and the place where they are going to fire their rifles.

In the case of Hamlet and the Balkan Hamletian, although their hometowns are remote, the murder they avenge is the same: that of their fathers. Hamlet questions how the blood seeker learned about the murder of his father, a question the Albanian does not understand. To clarify, Hamlet tells the blood seeker of the emergence of his father's ghost, who ordered vengeance. This information merely confuses the Albanian. The blood seeker tells Hamlet that he did not need any ghosts: everyone knew who had killed his father. The killer's name and house were well-known, as were the exact time and place of his father's death.

Aha, so it was not a secret murder, as in the case of my father's.

He must be mad and speaking in tongues. What is this stealth and poison? The *Kanun* does not recognize concealment. Poison, ropes, and knives offend the human body. The *Kanun* recognizes the rifle. The rifle does not insult, it merely kills.

So your father's killer did not hide anything.

Of course not. He declared the death himself. I remember, it was late afternoon when I heard the great cry: I have killed Llesh Mark; the body is by the mill road. The killer did not break with the *Kanun*. Everything was done beautifully.

Ah, was it so? What would have been said if he had not done it all so well?

The village would have criticized his rifle skills and the old men would have given him a penalty.

But I want to know: have you had disturbances of the soul, suffering, and doubts? Have you wondered whether this vengeance should be carried out? I am wearying of my own uncertainties. There are days when I think I am going crazy, which could well be true. I question myself and the words of the ghost.

I do not understand. I have never suspected anything. The *Kanun* lays it all out.

The conversation finally arrives at common ground: both men have delayed in avenging their fathers' blood, though for different reasons. The Prince for reasons that we know of; the mountain-dweller due to a girl. The Albanian burned with passion and wanted to get engaged before taking up the mantle of the blood seeker.

They admit to having suffered from the unbearable pressures exerted by the ghost and the *Kanun*. The ghost may have looked scarier, but the *Kanun* was much more terrible. The blood code was omnipresent: it lived in the village fountain, the basket of bread, the eyes of the girls, the mill, the church gate . . .

I suffered a lot, says the prince. Everything was so complicated. Denmark had become a prison. My mother was in bed with my father's killer. I was engaged.

The eyes of the highlander become cold again. He seems to regret the earlier confidences. His dark, old tongue returns to silence. This man does not understand the rules of the *Kanun*. Other things can be bent, but not the code. He must do everything correctly: he must utter the phrase before firing, taking aim correctly because he is only allowed one bullet; he must turn the body around, placing the gun next to the victim; he must declare the murder; and, finally, he must participate in the funeral of the deceased.

Here ends the impossible conversation between the prince of Jutland and the blood seeker. They both depart to their own affairs: one to the stage, where he acts out his story, and the other to an Albanian village, where he must avenge his father's murder. Once the Albanian man becomes "de-Hamletized," he removes the black armband from his sleeve and waits in the shadows for his turn to come. Another puts on the black armband. Weeks and maybe seasons will go by, until, suddenly, the familiar words are spoken and the bullet whirls. Another will perform the rites with his body and everything will be repeated again.

Let's return to Hamlet's interiority. That dark, desperately beautiful psyche. The inexplicable and nebulous prince.

The theory that all we see on stage is a manifestation of Hamlet's internal drama being played out seems attractive at first glance, but is nonsensical if considered in more depth. Every event portrayed in art, whether it be clear or vague, can be taken as a narrative of the inner psyche. All monologues and dialogues, whether ordinary or prodigious, are first experienced within our psyche. We may tell our friends about them after dinner and let these phrases die there, or we may channel them into our artwork, where they'll take on a new, more defined shape.

A psychoanalytic reading of *Hamlet* often places the Prince opposite an ancient model, that of Oedipus, and rarely, very rarely, opposite Orestes. A matricidal figure is preferred to a parricidal one because it better fits a Freudian reading. This preference has damaged the natural balance in the inseparable trio formed by Orestes, Oedipus, and Hamlet. This triad might be the most enigmatic, most beautiful, and anxiety-inducing ensemble in world theater.

Orestes most resembles Hamlet externally in the daylight, whereas Oedipus is an internal, nocturnal Hamlet. Orestes kills his mother transparently. He kills her for the state, the throne, and to avenge his father's death. After the murder, as though he were giving a press conference, Orestes justifies his crime before the citizens of Argos. Oedipus, on the other hand, murders his father in ignorance. He does not provide but requires an explanation. Driven by fatality, he walks toward the truth.

Hamlet is located between Orestes and Oedipus, which makes him more complex than both. Oedipus's crime occurs in a remote beginning that precedes the drama, Orestes's crime occurs in the midst of the drama, and Hamlet's blood feud occurs at the end of it. After murdering his mother, Orestes goes mad. Hamlet's madness takes on the form of a pretense. Oedipus escapes madness, but punishes himself by tearing out his eyes. Both Oedipus and Orestes survive their dramas, but they experience something worse than death: the pangs of conscience. Hamlet dies before experiencing these pangs. Of the three brothers, the youngest dies.

It would be hard to separate this trio. Orestes seems to us at first the most relatable, but Hamlet's wavering conscience makes him the most relevant. Between the two Greeks, we would choose, perhaps, Oedipus. The reason is purely an artistic one. The scaffolding of suspicion in *Oedipus Rex* has a sinister charm that fits the anxiety scenarios experienced by modern-day humanity.

When Oedipus realizes he has killed his father, it seems as though evil has reached its darkest point. But there is more. He learns he is sleeping with his mother. He is both her son and her husband. Evil does not stop here. Not only has he been a son and a husband to the same woman, he has also fathered children with her; impossible children who are also his siblings. Parricide. Incest. It is impossible to keep score of his transgressions. Son and husband to the same woman, Oedipus is a complete aberration.

The speculations surrounding Hamlet were mild at the start. The first, concerning his delays to avenge his father's blood, were almost noble. He has a gentle nature. He is only a student, hastily summoned after his father's death.

Did he really see the ghost of his father? Perhaps he is traumatized by the king's death and by the queen's hasty marriage.

He may have seen the ghost, but did he really talk to him?

Here doubts become less compassionate. Did he speak to the ghost? Did he hear the ghost's story, or did he invent it?

Here the speculations become accusations. Can you justify killing someone with a ghost's tale?

At this point, the yarn starts unraveling completely. Hamlet is not only an unjust killer, he is also a prolific one. He starts with Polonius and makes his way to his uncle, killing a total of five. What is this murderous rampage undertaken by the student from Wittenberg? What is his aim, and what he is trying to conceal?

Over time, our speculations grow more and more blackened, just like winter clouds. Did he participate in a conspiracy meant to overthrow the king, and is he now trying to make whomever witnessed it disappear?

But there is worse. Perhaps there was no ghost, and the only killer is Hamlet, the prince of Denmark, himself? Our Hamlet cataclysm finally ends here. Hamlet falls into darkness and reaches the end of the pit, where his brother, Oedipus, can be found.

Nothing is certain in this story. We can try to explain the development of the drama in another way. We can imagine, for example, a different ghost story. Instead of appearing to someone unconnected with his death, perhaps the ghost revealed himself to his murderer, as in *Macbeth* or *Julius Caesar*. Instead of the story we are given, the ghost might have asked different questions. He could have said, for example: Hamlet, my son, why have you done this to me, why have you killed me?

In his 2002 *Survey of Hamlet*, in an epilogue titled "What Happened in Elsinore," Pierre Bayard provides a narrative that is undoubtedly attractive. The event, according to him, goes as follows: King Hamlet has fallen asleep at the height of sinfulness, immediately after making love in the garden. His son, Prince Hamlet, approaches and kills his father—a crime that seems baffling at first. But there is no murder without a cause. Before going anywhere else, we'll turn to the woman with whom the king slept. She should still be by his side. She saw what happened. But she did not speak.

Who is this woman? Is it the queen, Hamlet's mother? For Freud's most naive students, the scene is simple. Hamlet, in an Oedipal rage, kills his father/rival out of jealousy. For more sophisticated thinkers, such an explanation is not credible. No matter how pronounced the Oedipal complex may have been in Hamlet, he must have known about his parents' amorous rites for years. Another woman must have driven the prince to his murderous fury. And this woman could have been none other than his fiancée, Ophelia. And so, completely out of his mind with shock, he murders his father. According to Freud, this act was carried out in primal clans by every son who rebelled against his father's claims of ownership over all the women. After realizing this, our reading of the Prince, just like our reading of Ophelia, changes completely. Now Hamlet is a hurt deer, hounded by psychoanalysts.

Hamlet is worse than a parricide. He kills not one, but three of his alleged fathers. First, he puts in the grave King Hamlet, his biological father. Then, suspicion leads him to kill Ophelia's father, Polonius. Polonius, old, wily, and distinguished, uses the girl to spy on the prince while also pushing her into the old king's bed. Polonius might have done so to gain influence in court, or perhaps, as is popularly suspected, the old man was sweet Queen Gertrude's former lover (the fact that before being killed he revolves around her bedroom as though he were in familiar surroundings reinforces this hypothesis). If this was true, then Hamlet may have been his son. As for Claudius, not only psychoanalysts but even the dispassionate Belleforest consider him Gertrude's old lover and Hamlet's third potential father.

The question of incest in *Hamlet* is a long-standing one. Some scholars have detected sexual tension between Hamlet and his mother. Others point out that if Hamlet is indeed the son of Polonius, then Ophelia is the prince's sister. Hamlet thus exceeds Oedipus, his Southern brother, in terms of his misdeeds, and is the first emblem of human decay.

Followed by hunters, the injured deer finally collapses. Its fate is determined. Hamlet emerges from literature only to end up on a ruthless autopsy table.

Psychoanalytic reading taken to an extreme loses both its credibility and its appeal. The accusation that Anna Akhmatova aimed at Freud, calling him the greatest pollutant of literature, was likely caused by a reading such as the one outlined above. The usurpation of literature, its transformation into a large psychiatric pavilion where doctors can examine a text like they would a disease, is an insidious deformation.

Homer was subjected to a similarly deformed reading long ago.

The sensational archaeologist Heinrich Schliemann's attempt to discover remnants of Troy took such a passionate hue that mankind forgot it was following the ruins not for the rubble, but for Homer's poems. The crux of the matter became distorted, and the ruins took the place of the poems. There even came a time when it seemed as though the questions and assumptions surrounding these excavations might affect the worth of Homer's poems.

Clear-cut answers were expected: Was this or was this not Troy? Was it a city, a capital, or a fortified town? Did Greek propaganda invent Troy to create a myth of a foreign enemy? Maybe Troy was simply a distant training grounds or a secret prison, like today's Guantanamo. But whether Troy was or wasn't, Homer remains Homer. He does not rest on geography, history, archeology, numismatics, seismology, or topography; he rests on poetry.

Let's call "topographic reading" the kind of reading carried out by land surveyors who, equipped with measuring instruments, look to determine the distance between the wall of Troy and the sea in order to find out whether the King of Troy could have made the journey to beg for his son's body on foot. When confronted by the duel between Achilles and Hector, a duel known for its tragic beauty, these readers focus on the perimeter of the ruins of Troy.

Yet it is not a sin to want a secondary reading that might supplement a traditional poetic interpretation. This duel between the two heroes of the *Iliad*, or more precisely my disappointment with it, pushed me to seek another type of reading years ago. I wanted to interact differently with the text not so that I could join the literary trend of breaking it down, but out of a sense of obligation to the grief I had felt upon seeing Hector's terror. I have returned many times to this scene, and my sadness, though somewhat diluted, is always there. Hoping to rectify something, in 1989 I proposed what I thought was a new reading.

Here is the scene, as given by Homer: Achilles, after his famous wrath, returns to war, and the Trojans are terrified. As he approaches like a black cloud, the defenders retreat behind the walls. The gates are closed. Only one man stands outside to greet him, Hector. Everyone has begged him not to do this. But he is the leader of the Trojans. He knows that Achilles is the better warrior, but Hector intends to fight to prove that Troy can do the impossible. He will fight the impossible giant in order to rise up against fate.

He announces this, and in front of the closed gate, he awaits the enemy. However, at the last moment, Hector feels terror. And then the worst evil takes place. Instead of facing his opponent and dying gloriously, as he had intended, he disgraces himself. He runs away with all of Troy witnessing his shame. Achilles chases Hector around the city walls three times. Finally, the Trojan prince comes to his senses. He fights and dies.

Even more surprisingly, the Trojans, who have seen Hector's disgraceful behavior, mourn their prince like a fallen hero. Not only is his glory unstained, but it even grows over time. It is as though the Trojans had completely forgotten his shameful attempt to escape. As though it had never happened. As though it were a mere hallucination.

A hallucination. That is exactly the right word. This was a hallucination that no one remembers because it was engendered by fear that was not theirs . . . it belonged to Hector.

It seems that what we think has happened is not what the Trojans saw from the walls. No doubt the Trojans, much like theatergoers, witnessed a magnificent spectacle, but what they saw was quite different from the description given by the Homeric text. There are two different vantage points: one is the view from the outside, from the walls, and other is the view from within, from Hector's fear. Apparently, the latter, interior view, is the true one. Troy continued to sing hymns to its leader because she never saw his shame. No one ever did, because Hector never ran before Achilles.

Hector falls to the ground from his first clash with Achilles. And on the ground, with his neck pierced cruelly, he has the first hallucination: he imagines running around the walls of Troy to escape death. After this, he has a second hallucination: his brother's shadow comes out to encourage him. Then a third: he breaks the spear during the duel, and asks his brother for another one. But the shadow of his brother is no longer there. There is only the wall and the closed gate. While Achilles is leaning over the body of the victim, Hector has his fourth and final hallucination: he begs that his face not be mutilated. Achilles then starts dragging Hector's body and, of course, also disfigures his face. From the walls, the Trojans witness the most unbearable scene: their prince covered by the clay of his homeland.

Of the four hallucinations, the third is the only one that corresponds with what the Trojans have seen. They have also seen Hector being dragged on the ground by Achilles, but by then the Prince's soul has already left its body.

In the Homeric text, the final hallucination is given at the start. This shift in order resembles the way in which dreams are constructed—that is, in such a way that the ending conditions the entirety of the narrative. Homer directs us toward this interpretation when in the midst of the duel between the two heroes he likens Achilles's pursuit to a dream. In this nightmare, Achilles can never reach Hector and Hector can never escape his pursuer.

The hallucination narrative, inevitably present in any interpretation of *Hamlet*, appears in almost perfect form from the beginnings of world literature. Shakespeare's interest in Homer was not accidental.

Albania was still communist when an old acquaintance, the prominent mythologist Pierre Vidal-Naquet, introduced me to his discovery regarding *Oedipus Rex*. We met in the summer during tourist season, in a hotel in Saranda. Some time ago, between the blue of the sea and the hotel patios, something strange had happened. The Albanian police had placed a dead body covered with a sheet on one of its motorboats, and then driven along the coast, slowly enough that people could be properly horrified by the fate of the victim, who, according to police, had tried to flee the country. The crowd gathered on the shore to watch the macabre display quietly. The bloodstains on the linen could be seen clearly. Many feared that the white sheet covered one of their relatives. The scene was repeated a few days later with yet another wretched victim. It was all reminiscent of ancient tragedies. The proximity of the Greek shores, just a few miles away, only encouraged this likeness.

The truth behind this fearmongering came out after the fall of communism. Covered by the white sheet had been a living soldier stained with fake blood. It had been the same soldier every time. The truth seemed even more macabre than the fabricated tale, and it was also even closer to the Greek theater.

When Pierre Vidal-Naquet spoke about his curious discovery, I had already heard the story recounted above. According to the mythologist, in 1585 in Vicenza, Italy, the tragedy of Sophocles had appeared not as *Oedipus Rex*, but as *Oedipus, the Tyrant*. Anyone living in the communist world would, understandably, be haunted by the question of whether tyranny was somehow essential to Oedipus.

Of the three princes, only Orestes and Hamlet have legitimate claims to the throne. However, only Oedipus ever becomes a king. Hamlet is killed and Orestes, though he is acquitted for killing his mother, is not quite considered a member of a royal family. Oedipus, on the other hand, is a liberator. He kills the sphinx, the great horror of Thebes. He is an unknown ranger with no royal lineage, but he becomes, or, more accurately, he is elected, king. He also becomes a tyrant.

Most tyrants follow roughly the same journey. They emerge as liberators, but then, once "elected," they become tyrants. Hamlet never presides over anyone, so we might call him an unrealized tyrant. Things remain vague where Orestes is concerned, and Oedipus is a consummate Hamlet.

The two men have similar attitudes about ruling over others. The fact that both King and Prince Hamlet bear the same name is a confusing one. Shakespeare was aware of Horvendill's resonant name, but he preferred, misleadingly, to use the same name for two characters. Perhaps Shakespeare was guided by the paradigm of Oedipus, who was, in a way, a son to himself, and the playwright might have wanted to create a Hamlet that was both the ruler and the ruler's offspring.

In 1585, sixteen years before *Hamlet*, there was a denunciation against Oedipus, the parricide, mother-violator, and destroyer of genealogy. The plague that gave the first sign that something was wrong in the kingdom of Thebes. People had sought the causes for the evil, until, slowly, it had come out into the open. It was the new ruler, the foreign savior, who had been so celebrated, that brought the plague. He had brought it because he had engaged in parricide and incest.

Did everyone believe that Oedipus was at the root of the plague that befell Thebes? Or were there those who suspected that it was not the parricide and the incest that brought on the plague, but something else altogether? Surely there must have been some skeptics. The human imagination is well-versed in comparing plagues with tyrannical reigns, and has been doing so from the time of Caligula to the current era of fascists. It is natural to ask, then, if the plague that struck Thebes might have been tied to tyranny instead of parricide and incest. Parricide and incest are, without doubt, great horrors. But the reversal of the fate of an entire people is more serious.

Given this, for years I have thought that a new reading of Oedipus is possible. According to this reading, Oedipus has not committed any of the crimes for which he is blamed. He did not kill his father and he did not sleep with his mother. He was guilty of a different crime, of the gravest, most apocalyptic crime—he became a tyrant.

But, as often happens in the conception of legends, when the human mind turns everyday phenomena, such as state taxes, into a dragon, we should realize that tyranny and the nature of the tyrant, both elusive concepts for simple minds, sounded much more tangible as parricide and incest. We thus have, through some metonymy, a replacement of Oedipus's crime. In addition, there is an element of time travel to his story. Not only is Oedipus not guilty of parricide and incest, he also did not commit some of the tyrannical atrocities he is accused of. Yet even this does not excuse him. Oedipus assumes, in the meantime, the role of the tyrant, which grants endless opportunity for crime. He may not have carried these crimes out, but if he had lived, he would have. He is a tyrant and has to be punished.

His father and mother are another point of irresolvable tension. Tyrants cannot have a natural origin. They breed one another from a barren, impossible mother. They borrow one another's psychosis, suspicions, and methods for choking populations. Stalin borrowed from Ivan the Terrible. The latter from Attila. Enver Hoxha copied Fidel Castro's paranoia.

The motifs of tyranny and oppressive natures prevail in Hamlet. The name shared by the father and his son remains inscrutable and brings this combination. Hamlet's words about his own tyrannical nature remain unclear. They can be explained, perhaps, by the same displacement that occurs in *Oedipus Rex*. If Oedipus committed the crime, Hamlet still needs to. He, too, is gripped by Oedipal conditionality.

The internal and external Hamlets seek to become one.

Prince Hamlet walks to the throne as though in a nightmare, balking at the idea of assuming power. This prince is not a great candidate for a tyrant. He is destroyed the moment he finally reaches the throne. After the murder of his uncle, the monarch, instead of chanting the usual "the king is dead, long live the king," he announces a new program: the king died, now let the prince die too!

Such a reading may resemble recent anti-communist or post-communist interpretations of *Hamlet*. The Polish scholar Jan Kot was one of the first to have provided such a reading. He describes the emergence of *Hamlet* in Krakow, in early 1956, a few weeks after the 20th Congress of the Communist Party met in Moscow, where Stalin's crimes were denounced. In the heated room, every remark has important connotations for the socialist viewers. Denmark is declared a prison. Poland, of course, was even more hopeless. Everyone spied on everyone else, there were hidden crimes, anxiety, expectations, and a ghost. To these people emerging from communism, *Hamlet* is the last tragedy of a reign. It is the expectation of another time.

With the exception of Russia, all socialist countries had dreamed of intervention and liberation in the form of an invasion from the West. The East Germans had expected this in 1954, the Hungarians in 1956, the Czechs in 1968, the Polish in 1981, and the Albanians for forty consecutive years.

During the '50s, special armed groups coming by plane from West Germany, England, or Italy would land by parachute in the high mountains of Albania. Their mission was to promote an insurgency that could topple the communist regime. But because of a betrayal that took place in London, perhaps the biggest treason that occurred during the Cold War, all of these envoys met tragic ends. Some did not manage to touch the ground. Hit from the bottom, they would die in midair, still attached to their parachutes. With snow blowing everywhere, they looked like the souls of the dead—but instead of ascending to heaven they were on a downward trajectory.

In Albania, as in Denmark, everything went backward.

Hamlet was published for the first time in Albania in 1926. For a country that claims to be a Hamletian region, this translation seems quite delayed. But things look differently if we remember the Ottoman ban on Albanian writing was only lifted in 1912, immediately after independence.

A language that was spoken but not written is quite different from others. Pent-up inside of it is the drama of incapacity, the longing to accomplish what is natural for every language: to create books. In the 1555 book *Missal* by Gjon Buzuku, half a century after the Turkish invasion, we see the phrase "longing for the printed seal." Many Balkan people have suffered from this longing. To the Balkan psyche, language is an indelible part of the nation's martyrdom.

In 1926, when *Hamlet* was translated into Albanian, the Albanian written language was merely fourteen years old. But like the witches of fairy tales, its youth hid a much older face: a thousand-year-old tradition of oral poetry and forbidden books.

Translation history in the Balkans, whether through oral interpreters or in books, was different from that of other places. To translate official discussions was quite dangerous. The Ottoman Empire carried out frequent talks with the prickly Balkan peoples. Like the characters themselves, these were quite hard. Their languages were difficult and misleading. Suspicion fell on translators from both sides. The renowned Italian maxim, "traduttore tradittore," here assumes its basic meaning. Interpreters were accused of treason and attacked by all parties.

The translation of *Hamlet* into Albanian seemed to strangely begin, somehow, with this.

"Is there Hamlet in this hall?" was an especially relevant question on February 23, 1924, when the eighteen-year-old blood seeker Beqir Valteri, as we know already, shot the future King Zog on the steps of parliament. Pale, with a revolver in his right hand, Zog walks toward the podium as members of both political wings take out their guns. As the hall freezes, he calls for peace. With the sixth sense of all great careerists, he can see that the bloodstains on his arm can accelerate his path to the royal throne. They wanted to kill him like Caesar, smack in the middle of the Senate, but they failed, and here he is, stronger than ever.

His cold blue eyes land hatefully on the opposition chief, Bishop Fan Noli. Surely, he must have ordered his murder. The dark eyes of the bishop never seem to leave him alone. He is forty-two years old and although he is the only one who does not keep a weapon, his bishop's coarse woolen cloth is much more dangerous than a gun. Zog has been spying on the bishop for a while. He knows that apart from the opposition, Fan Noli also runs the Albanian church. The bishop finds time for a third thing, something mysterious to many and conspicuously unrelated to his other occupations—the translation of an English drama. Everything the future king has learned about his political rival is true. Fan Noli was chief of the opposition, Archbishop of Albania, and *Hamlet's* translator.

The history of this translation is an incredible one.

Imagine an Albanian village. In the middle of the field, a woman named Marie Noli walks with a bag in her arms. Something moves inside the bag—a natural sight; it might be a lamb or a goat, perhaps a cat. After a long walk, the woman stops in front of the gates of the primary school, lowers her bag, opens it, and out comes a seven-year-old boy. The woman pulls his ear for having been mischievous and hands her rebellious son to the teachers.

This boy, who hated school so much that he had to be carried to class every morning in a bag, was Fan Noli, Albania's archbishop, the next chief of the opposition, the prime minister of the country after the overthrow of King Zog, a refugee after being overthrown by Zog, one of the most knowledgeable people in Europe, and a translator of both the Scriptures and of *Hamlet*.

Needless to say, his academic beginnings were not promising. Fan Noli confessed to his own surprising early stages. After finishing the Greek school (Albanian lessons were still banned), he took up jobs of all kind, such as horse tram exchanger in Athens, backup singer in a church in Constantinople, and line whisperer in theaters. He enjoyed the latter more than he had any of his other jobs. The theatrical troupes were nomadic and they played, among others, works by Shakespeare and Ibsen. Actors were illiterate, underpaid, and often went hungry. As a whisperer, Fan Noli was the only one who knew all the text by heart, and he served as a kind of dramaturge stand-in. Aside from their impoverished state, another anguish tormented the actors: troupe directors often quit after failed performances, leaving the cast on the open road, without food or shelter. The actors had to resort to begging, but it was not easy. Residents of small towns looked down on them, demanding explanations from the characters they'd played on stage. Hamlet, you prolonged your blood feud too much. You slut, they would address whomever played the queen. Their anger was so intense that sometimes they would beat the theater troupe.

In his memoirs, Fan Noli shows us that a secret link was being created between him and the great Shakespeare, who, after all, had also been an ordinary actor. It was not only the whisperer's role that was bringing him closer to the master; at times Noli also played the role of Hamlet. The archbishop tells us of one time when, as usual, the troupe had been deserted in a corner of the Balkans. Two key players, Hamlet and Ophelia, lay ill with a fever. Fan Noli was asked to play the role of the prince, and a replacement for Ophelia was surprisingly found. It was an old custom in the Balkans that beautiful girls in questionable occupations, such as acting, were accompanied by an unattractive sibling to safeguard her honor. Ophelia's sister, someone by the name of Kaliro, shy and withdrawn, admitted that she knew the role by heart after having heard it so many times. In fact, playing Ophelia was the main dream of her life.

Fan Noli spares himself in his own memoirs. He does not elaborate on what was happening in his brain when he whispered *Hamlet* for years in another language, Greek. Via his fascination for the drama he learned English, which allowed him to compare the Greek text with the original. Meanwhile, a third language stood waiting— his mother tongue, which he never learned in school because there was no school for it. He would one day give the Albanian language one of the most beautiful, if not the most beautiful, translations of *Hamlet* in the world.

On that cold day on February 23, 1924, in the hall of the Albanian parliament, Fan Noli experienced his own Hamletianness. In the Albanian parliament, posing the question "Is there a Hamlet in the hall?" would have elicited a very particular answer. That hall held murderers and future victims, blood seekers and ghosts, actors who played all of the above, and even translators.

Fan Noli, the only unarmed man, describes how everyone drew their weapons. According to him, the aged member of parliament, Aqif Kashahu, pointed a pistol with trembling hands at his own personal enemy, Vërlaci. Everybody else followed suit: they targeted someone . . . . someone, but who exactly? There is no evidence to prove where the barrels of the guns were pointed. It is unlikely that their direction was purely politically motivated. In an instant, all these deputies and ministers could become transformed into perennial blood seekers, because they each had some blood that they could seek.

They had renounced the *Kanun* because for years they were directing the fate of the nation. To uphold the laws prohibiting blood feuds, they had suppressed the ancient itch for blood. And then comes a moment of sudden liberation, when their thirst for revenge is put on display. What happens here is the opposite of what Hamlet is accused of—not a political crime masked as blood vengeance, but blood vengeance masked by politics.

Meanwhile, the tyrant Zog, as Noli would call him, signals for peace. The pistols are put away. The men morph from blood seekers to statesmen again. Aqif Kashahu has to give up on the old blood claim, older perhaps than he himself.

The assassin, meanwhile, is surrounded by guards. He not only surrenders himself, but, as though drunk, he begins to sing. The tyrant and the bishop continue to watch each other, clearly eager to plot the other's death. Both have plenty of experience with such intrigues.

Zog has been military chief since he was eighteen years old, and became chief of police at the age of twenty. The bishop has his own experience of violence, although it is of a different kind. Before acting and translating *Hamlet*, Fan Noli translated pieces of *Julius Caesar*. He was well-acquainted with Brutus.

What their eyes promised would come soon. Four months later, the bishop ousted his opponent through a coup. Zog retaliated and overthrew the bishop after five months. Fan Noli managed to escape Zog. Besides the effects of priesthood, he took with him the unfinished manuscript of *Hamlet*. He abandoned Brutus in order to become a Hamlet, and because Albanian self-importance knows no boundaries, soon he began to identify with Christ himself. He announced this publicly at some of his speeches during his exile.

While his opponents eagerly awaited his next move, Fan Noli did something that testified to his true greatness. With rare skill, he translated *Don Quixote* directly from the Spanish, which he learned for this purpose. The face of the frustrated knight was, apparently, his last literary mask. Later, as he prepared for death, he turned his back on translations of the liturgy and learned Hebrew at the age of sixty to try to reveal similarities between the Albanians and the Jews.

Fifteen years after he had expelled the archbishop, King Zog was also driven out by a tyrant, this time by an Italian one.

Like the bishop who carried *Hamlet* into exile, King Zog left with his wife, sisters, and his Hungarian nephew, whose father he had allegedly murdered, his own potential Hamlet.

The king and the bishop thus both ended up as migrants—a sad fate, which, on the eve of their departure from this world, led to a sort of indirect reconciliation. They died one after the other in the early '60s, one in Paris, and the other in Boston.

The third character of this story, Beqir Valteri, though younger than the others, was the first to die. He lived for sixteen years with the strange half-blood debt he owed the king. Zog neither demanded nor received the royal blood he was owed. The continuation of these theatrics reminded everyone of the ancient code. Though forbidden, the *Kanun* was still stronger than modern laws, and the King preferred to be called a tyrant than an offender of the *Kanun*.

King Zog continued to use the *Kanun* whenever he could. He justified his delicate decree that forbade Albanian Muslims from praying on their knees through the *Kanun*, which strictly prohibited Albanian men from getting on their knees. He also used the *Kanun* to refuse the request posed by "his precious friend Adolf Hitler," who asked that German troops be allowed passage through the land of Albanians, whom the führer claimed to "adore." Hitler's reaction to Zog's refusal is not known, but this denial did not stop the German regiments from entering Albania four years later, in 1943. By then, the king had already been ousted and Albania had a government of collaborators led by Mehdi Frashëri, a scion of the famous Frashëri family.

Incredible as it may seem, around this time the Albanian government dangerously justified refusing yet another of Hitler's requests through the *Kanun*. The Albanian government asked the German führer something that no one else had dared request; they asked that Albanian Jews be left untouched by the war. Correspondence discovered during recent years reveals that the Albanians made use of their besa to justify this request. In order to preserve their friendship with the Germans, the Albanian government asked that they be allowed not to turn in Jews so as to avoid violating their hospitality code. Hitler's reaction to this second invocation of the *Kanun* is also unknown. What we do know is that, although there were few Jews in Albania to begin with, by the end of the war their numbers had increased nearly tenfold—something that the Albanians have cause to feel proud about.

But let us return to the fate of the assassin who owed blood to the king.

In 1939, when the king left the throne and was exiled from Albania, Beqir Valteri thought he was saved. But fate decreed otherwise. After coming to power, the communists, instead of worshipping the would-be assassin, shot him. This seemingly illogical crime was never investigated. Apparently, since pulling the trigger came so easily to the communists, inquiring into the death of Beqir Valteri has been deemed not worthwhile. There were rumors that what cost him his life was perhaps the letter V in his surname, which he often doubled to spell his name a Germanic "Walter." If so, he may have been the only Albanian man killed over the duplication of a letter.

Albanian literature impatiently awaited the arrival of the ghosts of *Hamlet*. *The Oath*, a play written in the nineteenth century, inverted the Hamletian scenario: it was not the son who killed his father, but the father who killed the son. The drama was written by Sami Frashëri, whose brother Naim, after the death of another brother, had married his sister-in-law even more quickly than Gertrude and Claudius had married after the king's death.

Sami Frashëri was the third and youngest brother of a great Albanian house, but unlike in gloomy Scandinavian houses, this event did not produce any allegations of incest or crime. This was the south of Europe, with a different sun and different customs, thanks to which such a marriage would not have been dramatic unless something else, in this case the family's erudition, had not come along to complicate things.

Before it became a "great house," the Frashëri household was a temple of knowledge. The family spoke all major European languages, including Latin and ancient Greek. Such learnedness usually helps one overcome prejudices, but in this case their intellect, paradoxically, had the opposite effect. The great Frashëri residence was populated by images of ghosts from the past. Whether the tenants wanted to or not, they fell under the spirits' dangerous spells. Past events returned to memory, further aggravated by gloom and mystery. The rushed wedding and the widow's passing from one bed to another, which at first must have awakened only the curiosity of teenagers, eventually, after more reading, led to shocking murmurs around the porches of the great house. The younger brother, Sami, wrote the first and only drama that was born of these murmurs. But the story does not end here. The second Hamletian work this household produced was a novel titled *Navruz*. Born of the same impetus, this novel was written by Mehdi Frashëri, who, as mentioned above, became prime minister of the later puppet Albanian government. The hasty marriage might have remained unknown, like so many other great mysteries of that house, had not the troublemaker Faik Konica announced it in his newspaper, *Albania*.

The novel *Navruz* has as a protagonist an Albanian officer who, after being raped by women of the royal harem, like the Danish prince, leaves the abandoned Turkish capital in order to seek blood in Albania. Two other novels written in the 1930s, *Blood* by Ernest Koliqi, and *The Student at Home* by Millosh Gjergj Nikolla, sport similar motifs. The characters of the last two works are anti-Hamlets who disobey their ghost, namely, the *Kanun*. In Ernest Koliqi's *Blood*, an idealistic young teacher who believes in a Europeanized Albania opposes the code. But the demands of the ghost ultimately prevail, and he, in a semiconscious state, commits murder. In *The Student at Home*, the protagonist not only ignores the calls of the *Kanun*, he goes as far as to oppose them. When he catches his recently wed sister, toward whom he has uncertain designs, in the midst of committing an adulterous act, he not only pretends not to have seen anything, but secretly experiences satisfaction at the violation of the code. On such an occasion, the *Kanun* would have demanded the murder of the sinful woman.

During the communist years, when the *Kanun* was strictly prohibited, the motif of blood vengeance faded from literature. At a first glance, it seems odd that the bloody communist regime would be keen to challenge the *Kanun*, whose cruelty it shared. But with its Catholic roots, the *Kanun* was considered dangerous by the communist dictatorship. Its vision of death was quite different from the communist vision of death. For the *Kanun*, death was a fatal whorl: if blood is taken it must be repaid. The opposite was true for the dictatorship: the regime had the right to shed others' blood without giving its own.

The imposing code was targeted by communist propaganda using the same clichés that they used against the Pope, NATO, Hollywood, and Coca-Cola—lines that the Albanians hardly found convincing. After the fall of communism, Albanians returned to the *Kanun* with the same longing with which they returned to the dollar, NATO, the Pope, etc.

Throughout the twentieth century, *Hamlet* was, perhaps, the most popular literary work among the Albanians. Expressions like the famous "to be or not to be," which in Albanian reads as "to live or not to live," were widely used in everyday language.

Sooner or later, everybody has their own history with *Hamlet*, the author of this essay included. Around the age of twelve, after reading and copying *Macbeth* by hand and attracted by the word "ghost," I decided to transcribe *Hamlet*. But something stopped me. The end of the first act, which I liked incredibly, left me dumbfounded. I could not believe my eyes. Hamlet, after all the horror and supplication, was addressing his father's ghost without any honor. He called him uncle hedgehog and a drunkard shouting down the cellar. My disappointment knew no bounds. This Shakespeare, who I had been so impressed with, must have been completely crazy. I had detected some signs of his lunacy in meaningless words like "Hello, hillo, hillo, hawk come," but I had pretended not to notice. I could not take it anymore. I thought about throwing aside the book, never to open it again, but then I reconsidered. Perhaps I could fix this problem myself?

Until now I had not made any significant changes to the words of the author, and had occupied myself by simply recopying everything by hand. Yet I was convinced that after my discovery, the book was as much mine as it was Shakespeare's.

I remember the sunny winter day when I pulled the book off the shelf not to copy, but to alter for the first time. Others could do what they wanted, but I would have my own *Hamlet*. But it was not as easy to fix as it had seemed at first. A year ago, I would have amended the text confidently, but now I was more mature and when confronting the first serious issue in my life, I felt unsure. After many failed attempts, I returned the book to the shelf, feeling an unfamiliar void in my heart.

Years later, I remembered this incident while reading *Hamlet*, but found that I could not laugh at it as wholeheartedly as I wanted to. Later still, when reading about the endless controversies that surrounded Hamlet, with great surprise I noticed that some of them took issue with the dual and triple nature of the prince of Denmark. In short, Hamlet's mischievousness had started precisely there—in that first act that had so infuriated me as a child.

Before being diagnosed by mighty scholars, the prince's mischief and wickedness were discovered by hundreds of thousands of teenagers around the globe. But in our world the opinions of young boys and girls are not often taken into account.

What we so easily call the wickedness of Hamlet falls, apparently, at the core of the human world, that universal model the drama unfolds before us.

After the first words of the play—"Who's there? Nay, answer me: stand, and unfold yourself"—we await the answer to this question for hours. What comes after the scene is so vast that it relieves the agony of expecting an answer to the prior question and saves us.

Hamlet is a nightmare hidden behind clarity. A view given by some mirrors that break, in order to be reconnected again on the spot, and waiting to be mended again and again infinitely.

It is natural for the mind to return to Saxo Grammaticus. *Hamlet*'s misdeeds begin, perhaps, with this chronicle. And we can easily imagine William Shakespeare facing this weak chronicle that he was born to rectify, looking as horrified as if he stood before a devastation.

Researchers think that after the *Hamlet* he wrote jointly with the hapless Thomas Kyd, if that really did happen, it is likely that Shakespeare was unsure about embarking on a *Hamlet* of his own. In the investigations he was subjected to, Thomas Kyd was probably asked about his and Shakespeare's joint text. What were you trying to say with that drama, you and your friend, that roughneck?

After Kyd's death in jail, Shakespeare decided, finally, to order the muddled chronicle. Its promiscuity is disappointing. It is a Greek-Trojan chronicle but without Homer. It is the bloody tussle of the Atreus, but without Aeschylus. Saxo Grammaticus was chronicler of the state, writing at the bidding of the bishop of Denmark, Absalon. The mischief was, apparently, already there. And, perhaps it went even deeper. The original sin must be sought, perhaps, in the original ruins, the ancient sagas.

These sagas enjoy a permanent place of honor. They are considered magnificent, and everyone takes comfort in the fact that there will come a time in which to read and enjoy them leisurely. And since that time never comes, their status remains unchanged, when in fact, their worth is very far from what is thought. But such an opinion is likely to be called incorrect and people would rather not voice something so bound to be disagreed with.

Diamonds in the poetic old eposes are so few and so unconnected to each other that they seem to be scattered in a patch of sand.

Around 1600, William Shakespeare confronted this wasteland, and from a common story, he raised the highest skyscraper. It is disturbing, full of cracks and mysteries that are essential to its worth.

The genesis of *Hamlet*, Saxo's chronicle and the ancient sagas, is a model of mediocrity. For many scholars, its weakness started with the very names of the characters. We cannot expect anything good from Amleth, a name that means "indolent minds." In the Norwegian and Icelandic variants, the name means "to be out of one's mind," which is certainly no better. In short, stupid. Saxo Grammaticus, however, corrects all this in his chronicle. He describes Hamlet as a smart person pretending to be mad. Researchers have not clarified whether this duality comes from the ancient sagas, or whether is it mostly Saxo's creation.

From the start, Hamlet is double-faced. Or more precisely, he wears a mask over his face.

During the Chinese Cultural Revolution, many Chinese writers tried to defend themselves by feigning madness. It was the only way to escape Mao Zedong, a Chinese Feng a thousand times more sinister than the one from Jutland.

Shakespeare's Hamlet bears little similarity to Saxo's Amleth, and still less to the Amlod of the sagas.

In the chronicle of Saxo Grammaticus, we have the stalled story of a cunning man who behaves as though he were stupid in order to achieve his goal of avenging his father. Hamlet's wanderings around Denmark and England assume a special place in Saxo's forty-page chronicle, where, of course, only good things come to the prince from the king of England, who gives him his daughter as a wife, which would have certainly been a dream for readers of the time. If this were not enough, on a trip to Scotland Hamlet also marries the queen of Scotland, and the miserable, lonely prince ends up with two different women. There even comes a third woman, some

Hermrude, who loyally follows the prince to war, where he dies and she is taken by Hamlet's killer.

Saxo's chronicle draws attention to Hamlet's shield, which is nothing like the majestic shield of Achilles in *The Iliad*. Instead of the monumental sights depicted in the latter, this one contains only nonsense and wiles. Meanwhile, *The Iliad*'s shield captures a relevant artistic finding, the most beautiful in world art. According to the device, drawings or figures carved on shields are frozen inside of them and might spring out to intervene if needed. Aeschylus shows us such a fateful moment at the gates of Thebes, where Oedipus's sons battle to death.

In ancient literature, this artistic finding coincides with the emergence of another device, that of the ghost. The latter is found in Homer and, later on, in Aeschylus. Seneca, the writer who inherited the ghost to the Elizabethan theater, made use of more tangible spirits that appeared like nebulous scarecrows. For nearly two millennia, the ghost has preserved its dual nature as a mixture of the tangible with the intangible.

In Aeschylus's *The Oresteia*, we have both the tangible and the intangible ghost. When Orestes seeks to justify the murder of his mother, he shows us the bloody fabric that had served as a trap during the murder of his father, which may be seen as some fragment of his ghost. Later, the murdered Clytemnestra appears in the form of a genuine ghost.

Saxo Grammaticus does not have a ghost. Instead, Hamlet's hallucinations are frozen in the drawings carved on his shield. Shakespeare realized that these drawings did not suit the theater well, and did what the ancient Greeks had done two thousand years ago: he unfroze and turned them into a ghost.

The genius playwright realized that he was capable of doing what for others is virtually impossible: assuming a dual view on life. Unlike tyrants, who will do anything to acquire a second life, the genius experiences this duality naturally within himself. It is a part of him whether he wants it to be or not.

When Shakespeare built his magnificent *Hamlet* on the swamp of other chronicles' sad mediocrity or, in other words, when instead of a history of corruption he gave humanity a temple, he certainly could not have known that mediocrity would retaliate against him. This mediocrity chose as its target the earthly existence of the writer.

On the eve of his death, Shakespeare, it seems, had begun to anticipate the worst. The epitaph he wrote for his tomb reveals as much:

> Good frend for Jesus sake forbeare,
> To digg the dust encloased heare.
> Blest be the man that spares these stones
> And curst be he that moves my bones.

Exactly the opposite has happened. The stones and the bones were removed and continue to be destroyed to this day with ceaseless fury.

An impartial biography of his would look like this: In 1547, a certain Thomas Shakespeare, assumed grandfather of the playwright, is hung as a robber in his native town of Stratford. Hardly enviable beginnings for a biography. On April 26, 1564, "Gulielmus filius Johannes Shakspere" (William the son of John Shakspere) is born. On November 27, 1582, William Shaxpere is issued a marriage certificate to Anne Whately. The following day, November 28, 1582, William Shagspere, eighteen, lays a wreath at the church with Anne Hathaway, twenty-six years old. (There are more than fifty variants of his last name, which some interpret as a sign that he changed his name out of fear and guilt, like perpetrators do.)

In 1583 his daughter Susan is born. In 1585, the twins Hamnet and Judith, the psychoanalyst's next prey, are born. In 1594, a letter certifies that William Shakespeare (finally displaying the name we expect), along with two other authors, is given three twenty-pound notes for dramas written jointly. Hamnet dies in 1596 at the age of eleven. Hundreds of years later, psychoanalysts declare the boy the originator of Hamlet the character. In 1596, W. Shakespeare's name appears in documents of the tax office of St. Helena, London, for an outstanding debt of five shillings. On November 29, a bandit known as William Wayte files a complaint against William Shakespeare because the latter, together with a certain Francis Langlay and their respective wives, issues a "death threat" to the gangster. In November 1597, the tax office issues an advertisement: he has disappeared without paying the five shillings. In December of the same year, the municipality of Stratford requires ten pennies for a stone carriage commissioned by the playwright. In 1599, he publishes two sonnets. In 1600, Shakespeare wins the appeal against a certain John Clayton of Willington for seven pounds. That same year, his father, John, future prey of the psychoanalysts, dies. In 1610, John Donne calls him the British Terence. That same year, his daughter Susan complains in court that someone has called her a whore. On April 23, 1616, William Shakespeare dies. On April 25 he is buried in the church of St. Trinity Stratford, at first in an unnamed grave. A regrettable bust is placed next to the tomb. There is no mention of his tragedies, and, but for five notes, no script is left behind. In the frozen images we are used to seeing in countless textbook editions, a copper mask covers his real face.

It is almost incredible that this is all we know about the biography of the greatest Englishman on the planet—a few shillings in debt, some small claims court cases, two sonnets, an honorarium, and a stone carriage.

To supplement this meager tale, let's mention the seven facts that were omitted above:

His rush to get a marriage certificate on November 27, 1582, is inspired by his future father-in-law's threats, for some suspect that the groom may have impregnated Anne. In 1598, Shakespeare is sought by the London office of taxation for five outstanding shillings, along with a fine, for a total of thirteen. On October 6, 1599, he is again asked for the thirteen famous shillings. By 1601, as he works on *Hamlet*, the thirteen shillings have grown to forty. In 1604, there is a trial between the tragedian and a pharmacist in Stratford. In 1608, the name of William Shakespeare is marked as that of the godfather to the son of a trader in Stratford. In 1614, the municipality of Stratford gives him twenty pennies because a wandering preacher has stopped by his house.

This is the last fact of the expanded biography of William Shakespeare.

For lack of a better thing to say, let's repeat the word "incredible."

To make this more astonishing, let's compare all that we know about Shakespeare with what we know about one of his contemporaries, Peter Budi. Budi was considered a prominent writer in his country of birth, but was totally unknown to the rest of the world. Budi was born and died in a space that was Ottoman. As if this were not enough, he was a Roman Catholic parishioner, seemingly born precisely in order to be forgotten. First, his country, Albania, was conquered by the Turks and deleted from the map. Second, the religion he followed, Catholicism, was totally hostile to the Ottoman state. Third, Albanian writing was banned by decree. Fourth, and perhaps most important, he is a thousand times less important for world literature than Shakespeare.

Peter Budi was among the first to meld the Albanian language and Latin. Because of the prohibition of the Albanian language, this act would become common among friar writers like himself, who risked their lives by sneaking pieces of Albanian into the midst of the bundled Latin text. At the time, the dead Latin held, with its cold arms, a living language in order to protect it from death. Peter Budi covered an identity with his frock much like he hid one language within another. He lived writing books and plotting against the Ottoman state until, while he crossed the river Drin on a winter day, his aides, instead of helping him, drowned him.

Budi seemed marked to be forgotten. A preserver of an outlawed language and a threatened religion, with a homeland erased from the map, he was a real ghost. And yet he was not covered by the fog. Nobody doubted his existence, his name, or his work. One of his books, *Speculum Confessionis*, written approximately at the same time as *Hamlet* was, though infinitely inferior, has legitimate and more dignified origins than the famous tragedy. As the title indicates, the book is related to Catholic confession. After the Turkish invasion and the disappearance of local clergy, church services were held by foreign friars sent under Venice's protection. However, because these friars could not learn the difficult Albanian language, their ministering, including the confession, was done in Latin. But Catholic women in mountain areas refused to confess through an interpreter. The situation seemed hopeless. As if confessing their sins were not enough, now they had to deal with the added torture of confessing in Latin. And so, somewhat surprisingly, Budi created a book meant to help women become liberated from their sin.

We ascribe two lives to geniuses—the earthly life shared with other creatures and the life that has no body other than the geniuses' works. The life created by God seems, at first glance, the inviolable one. But surprisingly, it is not the life of God, but the artificial life created by the genius himself that is inaccessible to his detractors. However, detractors have long discovered that the earthly life is the only path through which evil, in the form of a virus or a bacterium, can overcome the more incorporeal life.

Sometimes geniuses, as though they had understood this, snapped their life into two—like amputating part of the body to save the rest. But in many cases this does not work.

Shakespeare stopped writing before he turned fifty. Perhaps he thought that this was a way to presage death, but the years dragged on, empty with the exception of those unpaid bills. In his will, he anticipated the worst. The havoc with his name, those fifty or so letter variations show this. Chacsper. Shaxpere. Sigiesberg (Germanic origin). Or Isaacsburg and Schachsburg (with Jewish roots). And the Arab variant, Sheikh El Arab origin Zubar, etc., etc. Then again the outstanding bills.

An endless torment, reminiscent of the duality between what is human and what is non-human in Gilgamesh's story, is inevitable in this case. And so is another critique of mediocrity.

Similar to the presence of a black hole and a thousand times more destabilizing than the specter of Elsinore, mediocrity has an infinite power. It seems tangible and easily dismissed, but it is insurmountable. Hypocritical and two-faced, it takes advantage of the ideals of equality, democracy, and human compassion, but in ages of total blindness, equipped with prisons and barbed wire, it can also turn tyrannical.

Art has a complex and unexplained relation with mediocrity. Mediocrity brings the stench of annihilation to art, yet without mediocrity art cannot function. Mediocrity's endless army of unknown martyrs provides millions of followers for art, who would otherwise never be seduced by great creators. However, in art, more strongly than anywhere else, mediocrity can turn into a monster.

The enmity between mediocrity and great art is so timeless that it is hard to pinpoint the true culprit. It seems easy to blame mediocrity, but art could just as easily be culpable. There is an enigma, something perversely fatalistic, inherent to great art. Something at its core goes against the current, against equality, and even against democracy. Thanks to this callous hierarchal elitism, art ensures its own superior stature. Try to remove this tyrannical crown and great art will fall.

Among the mandates of our world is the great rule that tyrants must fall. Tyrants that do not fall do nothing other than strain hopelessly against this fatal rule. While they do, they are doomed to endure the unbearable.

In Shakespeare's universe, fellow writers and would-be siblings sometimes emerge. Such appearances are rare because, of course, geniuses are rare. Geniuses do not come to his defense in order to calm his soul because they know that he does not need this. They come driven by some internal impetus from the family of geniuses: to reach closer to each other in infinite space when loneliness becomes unbearable.

Among the endless writings about *Hamlet*, we have occasionally mentioned James Joyce. Almost all agree that where the text of the tragedy is concerned, his is the best approach, but no one has gone beyond this assertion.

Indeed, Joyce, while speaking of Hamlet and his creator in the ninth episode of *Ulysses*, has done nothing but merely renew an ancient custom of the tragic Greeks. The idea is that geniuses of ancient times exchanged motives, stories, and even characters in the way that only family members can give and take their body organs—without the risk of rejection.

Joyce himself, having received the essence of his *Ulysses* from Homer, considered it natural to house *Hamlet* within it. The almost eighty pages about Scylla and Charybdis contain a discussion about Prince Hamlet, Shakespeare, Anne Hathaway, and the ghost, as though this were a natural family that belonged to our world. But this family consists of two people, Shakespeare and his wife Anne Hathaway, and two souls, Hamlet and his father's ghost. The least we could say is that this is an unnatural family.

Within this dual reality there is no dividing wall between our world and the world from beyond. Joyce uses all the opportunities that literature provides. Because Shakespeare sometimes played the role of ghost on stage, it is suggested that the ghost's appeal regarding the desecration of his marriage bed is really Shakespeare's lament over Anne Hathaway's desecration of their marital bed. Joyce mixes in other family members, dead kings, and poison only to end up in Anne Hathaway's bed, accompanied by startling phrases supposedly uttered by the playwright.

Joyce is aware of the deluge of commentary aimed at the genius, but he seems indifferent to it. When Shakespeare's very being is denied, Joyce's reading of *Hamlet* is the interpretation of a true brother that comes at a moment of deep loneliness. According to Joyce, of Shakespeare's two sons, the spiritual Hamlet and the physical Hamnet, the second would depart the world to make room for the first. This would only be the first blow fate dealt the playwright. Later, fate would become increasingly demanding, until it came to demand the impossible: the author's life.

The disappearance of Shakespeare's biography recalls the relationship between a life and an oeuvre. If life cannot bear the evils of the work, so the latter cannot bear the cloak of biography.

At a first glance, this disappearance seems a tragedy. However, from a more dispassionate viewpoint, the reverse might actually be true. The simplification and fossilization of biography can be taken as an escalation in the ritual consecration of genius.

Liberated from the annoying, coarse cloth of life, Shakespeare, with his dried bills on his hands, approaches his larger-than-life brethren. He approaches Homer, whose biography consists merely of his blindness, and Aeschylus, whose only known life events are his participation in the Persian War and his anger against Athens.

In accordance with the above model, about two centuries ago, illiterate Balkan elders, mostly Albanians and Montenegrins, although they had never read any of Cervantes, began to create another strange biography for the author of *Don Quixote*. The new biography, which shrunk outward facts, reads almost like a reverie Cervantes might have penned while trapped inside of a pirate's cave. By giving priority to dreams over life, Balkan elders, without knowing about Heraclitus, reiterated his idea that what appears to us in our sleep at night is a dream, and what we see in the daytime is death.

The destruction of Shakespeare's earthly life sums up the unnatural relation between a genius and humanity at large. It is more or less a rewriting of the story of Christ, where art takes the place of heaven and where Jesus ascended as a refuge after misunderstandings with the people.

We have come to the conclusion of this essay, and still cannot answer the question of whether this Hamlet is universal—and whether this universality would be a value or a flaw—definitively. The complications for the drama and the prince come apparently not from its hopeless beginnings, but from us.

We tried to remain distant from *Hamlet* and were not successful. We tried to claim it as our own and the drama, once again, was not obedient. We made it into our acquaintance, into a stranger, and into a part of our tribe. We claimed him for our era and declared him timeless.

There are times when it seems that we might finally be nearing its core: the prince. We run to become one with him. We all run together, whether princes, happy people, wretches, pacifists, or terrorists.

We show Hamlet our papers, credit cards, identification numbers, and masks. He observes them one by one, seems like he might be wavering, but as our hope grows, he throws them away one after another. We don't know what to do. We cannot bring him close, but are incapable of banishing him. He wants neither to meet nor to separate. Before we falter and say goodbye, we make a final effort. We remember that this world is not perfect and much in it is elusive. Perhaps he wasn't so careful and did leave a trace of himself behind for us. Just like beasts that leave tissue and membrane here and there, maybe he has left some part of himself somewhere. He left it because he knew that he still held the only key to the essence of his secret, which we could not hope to decipher even if we found what had been left behind.

Perhaps instead of leaving his key among us people, he encoded his true semblance among other creatures, among the deer, or the trees, with which he has often been compared, especially those that have been burned down. We soon realize that this is but a fanciful flight, a poetic longing, that does not take us very far.

Whether willingly or unwillingly we are reminded of our humanity. Once again, we seek to discover Hamlet's riddle in its midst. We retrace our steps. We search for the effects and pieces he might have left behind in the northern hamlets, or the islands of the Mediterranean, or in the Caucasus.

What might have been left behind carries not the Hamlet of the stage, but a pre-Hamlet, primal and rude. We have greater hopes of learning something from these objects than from the trickster on the stage. We seek to understand what the difficult prince wanted, the impossible thing we could never grasp. Perhaps he wanted to return to his origins, to the gray waterfall of mediocrity that gave rise to him. It is likely that the latter, as the mother who wants her mad bastard, is looking for him, too. Both parties longingly and sadly seek each other through the dunes, reeds, and sand. We have suddenly become an extraneous third party and feel foreign to this story.

Six years after reading and trying to repair *Hamlet*, I met his refracted image.

It was the autumn of 1954, and Albania had been communist for ten years. As any student recently arrived in the capital, I was amazed at its curiosities. One of its most nebulous and seductive surprises had to do with *Hamlet*.

I did not understand this in the beginning. There were pale wanderers who did not remind me of anyone in particular. They walked through the capital streets in northern highlander attire and with an axe in their hand. Their eyes were cold and so were their cries, as though they came not from a human throat or language.

I learned very quickly that there was nothing surprising to them. They were highlanders who had come down from the mountains to perform a simple job: to cut wood that families of the capital needed every season for their stoves.

Later, I learned that this was merely the outer layer of their appearance. There was another, deeper layer. These people who came down from the mountains were for the most part blood seekers who had refused to participate in the blood feud. As a result, the rough Albanian *Kanun* had them deleted from all population registers of the world.

But this was not the worst. They could no longer be called a "man" and could not respond to the traditional greeting of "are you a man?" with anything other than silence. In short, their loss was unbearable. They left behind a population of dead relatives, who were different from the ordinary dead. These were the blood losers, people who were called lost souls. It was not their fault, of course, but they were punished just like the unbaptized people in Dante's first circle of hell.

Woodcutters knew this, and in all of their behavior, walking, words, and loneliness they looked like they were from another world.

They were failed Hamlets. Lost residents of the highlands who, without knowing anything about Goethe, Coleridge, or hundreds of others, had one day been thrown out of the only system they knew: the *Kanun*. They had done what four hundred years ago Hamlet had not been able to do in the theater of London, in the chronicle of Saxo Grammaticus, or in the original Icelandic sagas.

The story of Hamlet is about how mediocrity is bred, which leads us to realize that mediocrity has its share of import in either the destruction or the immortalization of great art.

The parallel story of Hamlet continues its life in books and in the theater. It is endless, like the gusts that circumnavigate the planet, and is guided by a core that is still unknown to us.

Here's a startling scene that took place at the beginning of twenty-first century. It is 2006. We are in Albania again, this time after communism. There is a trial in the Accursed Mountains. The first act. The first session. Judges, lawyers, guards, witnesses, the prosecutor, and the defendant for murder come on stage. **Judge:** And now, defendant, explain what happened to the court: your crime, reasons, and whether you repented. **Murderer:** Your honor, I ask forgiveness and mercy. I will take the full extent of my sufferings to my grave. Every night the ghost would appear. Avenge my blood, he said. I can't rest until you kill Cuf Kërtalla. **Attorney (interrupts):** What says this rogue villain? What ghost, you joker? **Murderer:** The ghost of Shuk Shkreli, Mr. Prosecutor, my maternal grandfather, may he rest in peace. He appeared every night, like the ghost of Hamlet. **Prosecutor:** Oh, good God, what Hamlet are you talking about, you sly one? **Lawyer (intervenes):** Gentleman of the court, the prosecutor is reviling the defendant. My client is referring to Shakespeare's Hamlet. **Prosecutor:** Sirs, I am astounded that he even knows who Shakespeare's Hamlet is. You killed Cuf Kërtalla over the hundred and twenty thousand euros that he wouldn't give you. I know about the dirty business you had between you, the trafficking of drugs, women, and Kurds, and now you tell us about the ghost of Hamlet. **Attorney:** Gentlemen of the court, please censure the prosecutor for insulting my client. **Judge:** Opposition rejected. Defendant, continue. **Murderer:** Every night, the ghost appears: kill Cuf Kërtalla, he told me, kill him, like he killed me.

There are whispers in the hall. The correspondent of the local newspaper writes "Accursed News" across his notebook. The trial becomes more difficult than expected. Even the Council of Europe has made remarks about the Albanian *Kanun* and about the lawyers who are apparently advising local Albanian bandits to justify their crimes through Shakespeare's *Hamlet*.

Whispers in the courtroom continue. We are back to the ghost. Whose ghost? Some Hamallat, it seems. I heard another name. A Shukaspir. God willing, he is not from these parts. It doesn't sound as if he is. I heard another name: Checsper. I heard Shaxpere. By God, the name changes from moment to moment like Satan's name. Sigiesberg. Schachsburg. Isaacsburg. Sheikh El Zubar.

The thundering murmurs drone on. The story of Hamlet and his creator is one of perpetual misunderstanding. It was like this when he was first born in London, and so it has remained ever since.

We have nothing left but to return to the castle of Elsinore, where amid the fog, on the eve of the emergence of the ghost, we revisit the drama's first words, which demand a tangible presence and self-identification.

According to Joyce, these words were not really directed at the ghost of the play; they were meant for the play's enigma. Through the screen of death, the ghost speaks to his son, it speaks to us all.

Meanwhile, the ghost is raging. It is both there and not there like Shakespeare himself, who must pledge to leave one life in order to save the other.

According to Joyce, Shakespeare is the prince and ghost. He is everything. He is a hybrid who lives in between worlds.

The ghost never mentions the sky. Its urgency never has anything to do with ascending to heaven, but instead with a descent to the ground.

It can be said that this is, perhaps, the burden of the prince. And this might be the essence of the history of Hamlet, who lived at a time not so far from that of Jesus Christ, but who, unlike him, could not ascend to heaven, and remained among us.

(PARIS, DURRES 2005–2006)

ABOUT THE AUTHOR

ISMAIL KADARE, considered one of the greatest authors in world literature, was born in Gjirokastra, Albania in 1936. As a boy, he witnessed World War II, the occupation of his country—by fascist Italy, Nazi Germany, and the Soviet Union—until 1944, when the communist dictatorship of Enver Hoxha was established in Albania. At the age of seventeen he won a poetry contest in Tirana, earning him an authorization to travel to Moscow and study at the Gorky Institute, from which he was expelled in 1961 because of the break in relations between the Balkan state and the USSR. While attending the Muscovite institute, he wrote *The General of the Dead Army*, which was enormously successful in France. Thanks to this novel, he obtained a sort of immunity in his country for representing national pride, even though he did not submit to communist dogmas. Compelled by the regime, he became a member of the Albanian parliament from 1970 to 1982. In 1990, a few months before the collapse of the dictatorship, he exiled himself in Paris, the city where he has lived since, although he visits Albania frequently.

A great scholar of Albanian traditions and the idiosyncrasies of this Balkan state, his works take place around various incidents in his history, such as the break between Albania and the USSR, *The Great Winter* (1977); Catholic and Orthodox rivalries, *Doruntine*

(1980); and the split between Tirana and Beijing, *The Concert* (1988). One of the most typical features of his work is that it is permanently open: Kadare will rework his writings, poems become stories, stories grow and become novels and these, occasionally, will be reduced to stories. Another characteristic is how he recaptures humanity's great concerns and debates, taking them from oral tradition and classic literature, from Aeschylus, Homer, Shakespeare, Cervantes, and Chekhov, and placing them within a contemporary context.

However, the central theme of his work—expressed in each of his books—is totalitarianism, its mechanisms and the complicities that make it possible. This literary obsession reaches its climax in *The Palace of Dreams* (1993), published in Albania in 1981, when the communist dictatorship still governed. In this work, the Albanian writer builds an immense parable on despotic perversion, where in an imaginary country a mammoth machine at the service of absolute power, the Office of Sleeping and Dreaming, controls the dreams of its citizens. Despite the fall of communism, Kadare continues to give voice to the soul of totalitarian societies, such as in *Three Elegies for Kosovo* (1999) and *In Front of a Woman's Mirror* (2002). His latest releases are *Life, Death, and Representation of Lul Mazreku* (2007), *Agamemnon's Daughter* (2003), and *The Successor* (2005).

He is a member of the Academy of Moral and Political Sciences of Paris, one of the five that make up the Institut de France, a member of the Berlin Academy of the Arts, and an officer of the French Legion of Honor. In 2005, he received the International Booker Prize. In addition, he received an honorary degree from South East European University (Republic of Macedonia).

ABOUT THE TRANSLATOR

A native Albanian, **ANI KOKOBOBO** is assistant professor and director of Graduate Studies in the Department of Slavic Languages and Literatures at the University of Kansas, where she teaches Russian literature and culture. She has published an edited volume, *Russian Writers and the Fin de Siècle—The Twilight of Realism* (Cambridge University Press, 2015), and has a monograph forthcoming, *Russian Grotesque Realism: The Great Reforms and Gentry Decline* (Ohio State University Press, 2017), as well as another edited volume, *Beyond Moscow: Reading Russia's Regional Identities and Initiatives* (Routledge, 2017).

RESTLESS BOOKS is an independent, nonprofit publisher devoted to championing essential voices from around the world, whose stories speak to us across linguistic and cultural borders. We seek extraordinary international literature that feeds our restlessness: our hunger for new perspectives, passion for other cultures and languages, and eagerness to explore beyond the confines of the familiar. Our books—fiction, narrative nonfiction, journalism, memoirs, travel writing, and young people's literature—offer readers an expanded understanding of a changing world.

Visit us at www.restlessbooks.com.